IMAGES OF Ⅴ

AIRCRAFT SALVAGE DURING THE BATTLE OF BRITAIN AND THE BLITZ

RARE PHOTOGRAPHS FROM WARTIME ARCHIVES

Andy Saunders

Pen & Sword

AVIATION

First published in Great Britain in 2014 by
PEN & SWORD AVIATION
An imprint of
Pen & Sword Books Ltd
47 Church Street
Barnsley
South Yorkshire
S70 2AS

ISBN 978-1-78303-040-8

Typeset by Concept, Huddersfield, West Yorkshire HD4 5JL.
Printed and bound in England by CPI Group (UK) Ltd, Croydon CR0 4YY.

Pen & Sword Books Ltd incorporates the imprints of Pen & Sword Archaeology, Atlas, Aviation, Battleground, Discovery, Family History, History, Maritime, Military, Naval, Politics, Railways, Select, Social History, Transport, True Crime, and Claymore Press, Frontline Books, Leo Cooper, Praetorian Press, Remember When, Seaforth Publishing and Wharncliffe.

For a complete list of Pen & Sword titles please contact
PEN & SWORD BOOKS LIMITED
47 Church Street, Barnsley, South Yorkshire, S70 2AS, England
E-mail: enquiries@pen-and-sword.co.uk
Website: www.pen-and-sword.co.uk

Contents

Acknowledgements

The photographs contained in this volume are largely from my private archive of images I have collected of Luftwaffe aircraft downed in Britain during the period 1939 to 1945. A great many friends and colleagues have assisted me in this quest, have helped me identify the scenes captured on film, or otherwise provided additional information. In no particular order of merit, I would like to thank: Peter Cornwell, Steve Hall, Chris Goss, Dennis Knight, Winston Ramsey, Richard Hukins, Dave Buchanan, Phillipa Hodgkiss, Alfred Price, Gerry Burke and Martin Mace.

In addition, I must mention two other fellow researchers who are no longer with us but whose work added considerably to our sum of knowledge relating to the recovery of aircraft wrecks in wartime Britain. They are my late friend Pat Burgess and a colleague of many years, Peter Foote. Pat had been a prodigious collector of information relating to the county of Sussex, the area in which much of the activity described in this book had taken place. Peter Foote had been equally industrious in recording the minutiae of events during the Battle of Britain and the Blitz across Britain since the late 1940s and his tireless research work has left a legacy of unequalled information. Had he not recorded some of these events before it was too late to find the evidence then our knowledge of that period would be much the poorer.

Lastly, I must pay tribute to the late Arthur Nicholls. His gift to me of his surviving records, reports and photographs provided a veritable treasure trove of information.

In addition, I must extend my thanks to the many other individuals and organisations that have assisted me in over forty years of related research who I have not named here. My thanks to you all.

Andy Saunders
September 2013.

4

Introduction

Clearing away the debris and detritus of modern mechanised warfare is something that warring nations have had to deal with since the end of the First World War, and the inevitable result of twentieth century warfare was the large-scale littering of land and sea with the wreckages that combat left behind. The massive and widespread land battles across Europe during the first and second world wars left their own particular trails of destruction and debris that had to be cleared away before normal life could once again resume in the post war periods, and those clear-up operations presented their own challenges, dangers and difficulties. In the British Isles during the Second World War, and for the first time in modern history, the country was faced with widespread destruction caused by bombing, and disruption and damage to infrastructure caused by almost six years of conflict – some of that damage resulting from defensive measures taken by the military with the establishment of aerodromes, fortifications and other defences.

Putting things back to how they were took very many years, although during the 1939–1944 period itself a far more immediate problem faced the authorities in Britain: the collection and disposal of shot down or crashed aircraft, allied and enemy. Such crashes needed almost immediate attention for a variety of reasons. How were they dealt with, and what subsequently happened to them?

Often the remains were badly smashed up or even largely buried in the ground, but they could yield useful clues about new enemy developments such as advances in weaponry or armour, improved engine installations, the quality of oils and fuels used, information about factories where component parts had been built, as well as the significance of German tactical markings, camouflage paint schemes and even unit emblems. Additionally, much could be discovered about the effect of British munitions against enemy aircraft. In some cases these German aircraft were substantially intact and a few prime examples were selected for public display for fund raising and morale-boosting initiatives and many of these are illustrated in this book. Others that were deemed of greater use or value were subject to careful dismantling and transportation to the Royal Aircraft Establishment, Farnborough. Here, a more thorough technical examination was possible and some examples were then further earmarked for full repair and refurbishment and an eventual return to the air for flight testing. Much could be learned about the flying characteristics of these captured Luftwaffe machines, including the strengths and weaknesses of various types as they were assessed against British fighters and thereby give RAF pilots and other defending forces a better insight into the enemy aircraft they were pitted against. To keep these captured examples airworthy, a plentiful supply of spare parts could often be gleaned from other crashed aircraft of the same type that were falling onto British soil on a somewhat regular basis.

British aircraft needed to be dealt with too. Very often, as with the German types, the wreckages were smashed up, burnt or perhaps buried. The remnants still had to be cleared away, although there was a somewhat different agenda in that process. Clearly, the crashes held no intelligence value and it was simply a case of taking away the wrecks from wherever they had fallen. Often, RAF aircraft had been force-landed and were assessed to be repairable for eventual return to flight and it was thus essential that they were dismantled as carefully as possible without causing any further damage. More seriously damaged machines might yet yield salvageable parts and equipment that could be returned to stores for use and this was part of the remit of the RAF Maintenance Units charged with retrieving such wrecks. However, many of the more smashed-up wreckages would eventually follow the same route as the demolished Luftwaffe airframes; processing for scrap and smelting into ingots.

Given the scale of wartime aircraft losses over the United Kingdom, a network of RAF Maintenance Units across the country were allocated regional responsibility for the collection and disposal of aircraft wreckages. Sometimes, and especially during the hectic summer of 1940, the RAF were unable to keep pace with the volume of work as more and more aircraft were being brought down, and the Air Ministry consequently engaged civilian contractors to collect and transport British and German aircraft wrecks. Detailed arrangements were also put in place for the guarding, inspection, collection and disposal of wrecks, and specific protocols were firmly established for dealing with the growing number of crashed aircraft.

This book looks at what is a particularly fascinating aspect of the Battle of Britain and the Blitz through a remarkable collection of unique photographs. It is a story that has never before been fully told.

To present day aviation historians and researchers, the work of the wartime aircraft salvage gangs is often a matter of great interest, despite the fact that little has been written on the subject. The work of the RAF's Maintenance Units in clearing wrecks in south-east England during 1940, supported by civilian haulage firms who were contracted by the Air Ministry to assist the RAF gangs in wreck recovery and clearance, represents an important aspect of the history of the Battle of Britain.

When an RAF aircraft did not return from a training or operational flight its parent unit had a duty to notify the Air Ministry, who in turn informed the Headquarters of No. 43 Maintenance Group, located at Cowley near Oxford. If it was known that the aircraft in question had crashed or made an emergency landing in the UK, the staff of No. 43 Maintenance Group would pass on this information to the RAF Maintenance Unit (MU) that covered the area in which the aircraft had been lost. The airframe or wreckage would then be inspected by the MU's crash inspector, and following this suitable arrangements would be made for its collection and disposal.

For enemy aircraft the procedure was different. The first step in the process was an inspection by an RAF Technical Intelligence Officer from the A.I. 1(g) department – the A.I. standing for Air Intelligence. This individual's task was to garner as much information relating to the aircraft in question as was possible. Identification markings, type of engine(s), armament, armour plate, crew number and details, leading edges (and specifically whether protected against balloon cables by cutters, strengthened, or fitted with other devices, including de-icing equipment), and, lastly, recommended disposal – these were just some of the questions on his form, known as 'Form C'. Once this had been completed, and all relevant details of equipment and identification had been noted from the aircraft or wreckage, then it could be released for recovery by the relevant MU.

The brunt of responsibility for the clearance of wrecks, both British and German, in the main Battle of Britain areas of Kent, Sussex, Surrey and Hampshire during 1940 fell to No. 49 Maintenance Unit. Located at RAF Faygate near Horsham in Sussex, and with its parent unit being RAF Tangmere, an advance party had arrived to establish the base there on 28 September 1939. The establishment at Faygate was initially named No. 1 Salvage Centre, but the title was formally changed to 49 Maintenance Unit on 21 October 1939.

Situated beside the main London to Horsham railway line the site grew into a collection of wooden huts, dominated by a canvas Bessonneau type hanger and a sprawling and ever expanding dump of wrecked aircraft. Few domestic facilities were provided at the site and therefore all of the personnel were billeted with families in the nearby town of Horsham.

One of those who subsequently recalled his time with 49 MU was Leading Aircraftman Monty Cook. His overriding memory of his time as a '49er' was the discovery of bodies or body parts at a crash site. At one location, for example, he pulled a boot from the wreckage of one aircraft only to discover that the foot was still inside it. 'I went and found a spot by a tree where the sun was shining and buried it there,' he remembered.

Apart from the few personnel who remained permanently on site at Faygate, under the command of the unit's Commanding Officer, Squadron Leader Goodman, most of the airmen were divided into Crash Parties of eight to ten men, with each group being under the command of a senior NCO. At its peak, 49 MU could muster fifteen of these teams. In addition, the unit had a number of Crash Inspectors, mostly of Pilot Officer rank, who visited each aircraft to be recovered and assessed any particular problems and decided on equipment and manpower required for the recovery task.

Not to be confused with the MU's Crash Inspectors were the Intelligence Officers of Air Intelligence mentioned previously. One A.I. 1(g) Officer was attached to each MU in order that each part of the country could easily be covered, rather than rely on officers working from the A.I. unit's H.Q. that had been established in a converted school in Harrow Weald.

With the unprecedented level of aerial activity over the United Kingdom in the summer months of 1940 it soon became obvious that the existing chain of MU bases around the country could not cope with the large and increasing numbers of wrecked aircraft littering the countryside.

Perhaps feeling the strain the most was the hard-pressed 49 MU. The situation was not improved when the unit lost a number of vehicles, including a Ford V8 staff car and a Commer low-loader, during the *Luftwaffe* attack on Hawkinge on 12 August 1940. This was followed by the death of two drivers and the loss of three Commer low-loaders, a Coles crane and a Bedford three-tonner during the devastating Stuka raid on RAF Tangmere on 16 August 1940. Something needed to be done and prior to the formation of 86 MU at Sundridge, Kent, in early 1941, to help ease the burden on 49 MU, the Air Ministry also engaged a number of firms of civilian contractors from the road haulage industry.

Among the civilian companies employed to assist the RAF were Coast Transport Ltd, Portsmouth Carriers and Messrs A.V. Nicholls & Co. The latter company operated from its business premises at 100 North Road, Brighton, but, in terms of aircraft salvage, came under the direct control of 49 MU at Faygate.

Unlike the RAF recovery parties, those of Messrs A.V. Nicholls and other civilian firms consisted of untrained men working with little equipment and often under conditions of extreme difficulty. Usually only two men were despatched on a recovery job and might be expected to dismantle, cut up or dig out a wreck depending on the circumstances of the crash.

Basic equipment for the A.V. Nicholls recovery party would be a pair of sheer legs, oxy-acetylene cutting equipment, buckets, spades and a lorry with a flat-bed trailer. Mr Jack Austen and Mr Bob Sawyers performed most of the eighty-odd recovery jobs undertaken by the A.V. Nicholls between September 1940 and March 1941, from which date the civilian contractors ceased to operate due to pressure having been eased by the formation of 86 MU at Sundridge, Kent, and by a comparative lull in aerial activity.

Fortunately, the records relating to the activities of A.V. Nicholls & Co. during 1940 have survived and were passed into the safe keeping of the author by the late Mr Nicholls in 1976. They provide a fascinating insight into this aspect of Battle of Britain history and have enabled historians and researchers to solve a number of mysteries relating to downed aircraft from the 1940 period.

Notably, one report in the Nicholls file, relating to the loss of a Spitfire I, X4278, enabled the Ministry of Defence and Commonwealth War Graves Commission to place a named headstone on the grave of Pilot Officer John Cutts of 222 Squadron who had been killed when he was shot down by a Messerschmitt Bf 109 over Maidstone at 13.30 hours on 4 September 1940. For some reason the casualty recovered from Spitfire X4278 had not been identified and was buried in 1940 as an 'unknown airman' at Bell Road Cemetery, Sittingbourne, but a report in the archives of A.V. Nicholls & Co. identified the serial number of the Spitfire in which Cutts had been lost and, thereby, provided a definite link to the grave of the previously unidentified pilot who had been recovered from that wreck in 1940.

One problem frequently encountered was the wholesale removal of souvenirs from crashed aircraft by military and civilian gangs alike. Such was the level of the problem that the Minister for Aircraft Production issued a statement on 6 October 1940 urging the public not to remove material or equipment from crashed aircraft. This was later followed by the issue of Standing Orders covering the Guarding and Salvage of Crashed Aircraft, in which the subject of souvenirs was also dealt with.

None of this, however, did anything to prevent 49 MU's CO, Squadron Leader Goodman, from having to issue a letter to the tenant of Cooling Court, Cooling, Kent on 7 October 1940, requesting that the bearer of the letter, Jack Austen, be handed parts of a German bomber in the farmer's possession. The aircraft in question was a 9/*KG* 77 Junkers Ju 88, Werke Nummer 5104 and coded 3Z+DT, which had been shot down at Cooling Court on 18 September 1940. It would seem that very little heed was paid to this formal demand. When the author visited Cooling Court in 1979 and interviewed its owner, a Mr Whitbread, and showed him a copy of the letter of 7 October 1940, a smiling Mr Whitbread promptly disappeared into his attic. He emerged a short while later with armfuls of relics from the Ju 88 in question – including fuel pumps and filters and a complete elevator trim tab!

Apart from the problems of recovering items like these from souvenir hunters the salvage gangs sometimes had other headaches or dangers to contend with. For example, whilst cutting up the wreckage of Heinkel He 111, Werke Nummer 3322, 1H+GP, of 6/*KG* 26, which had been shot down at Gordon Boys School, Chobham, Surrey on 24 September 1940, ganger Bob Sawyers caused a large grass fire with his cutting gear which, in turn, detonated scattered rounds of 7.92mm ammunition.

Another excavation which caused problems was the attempt to dig out, by hand, Pilot Officer W. Armstrong's 74 Squadron Spitfire IIa, P7386, from where it had been shot down on 14 November 1940 – Armstrong had baled out over Dover at about 14.00 hours after combat with German fighters. Superficial surface wreckage was cleared by Austen and Sawyers on 25 November and excavations down to a depth of fourteen feet were made. At this level the fuselage and cockpit wreckage were recovered. At fourteen feet, however, the engine had not been located and the recovery work ceased. Not satisfied with the outcome, Squadron Leader Goodman ordered that digging operations should continue and work re-commenced on 25 November to a depth of some twenty feet where the engine was finally located. At this depth, water began to flow into the excavation and despite the use of a pump the engine could not be extricated from the wet soil and just sank deeper. Eventually, the team had to admit defeat and the recovery work was halted on 2 December when the hole was filled in on top of the unrecovered engine.

To some, the reports about the two men digging to twenty feet by hand and recovering all of the buried Spitfire's wreckage apart from the engine might seem a little far-fetched. However, apart from there being photographic evidence of the salvage gang at work, the crash site was again excavated in October 2011 and the buried Rolls-Royce Merlin XII engine was recovered from around twenty feet – just exactly as the Nicholls gang had reported.

Another example of the dangers involved in wreck salvage is provided by the work undertaken in relation to the Dornier Do 17 of 8/KG 3, (werke number 2573 and coded 5K+CS), which had crashed into the gardens of houses in Wansunt Road in the London Borough of Bexley on 3 November 1940. Having been despatched to the site, the Nicholls gang had a lucky escape when a stick of bombs fell across the crash site during the night; thankfully no-one was present at the time. When they returned the following morning, Nicholls' men were greeted with a scene of utter devastation. Amongst other damage, one of the Dornier's Bramo-Fafnir engines had been thrown by the exploding bombs into the cab of the gang's Leyland lorry.

On another occasion, two RAF maintenance unit airmen were electrocuted at Studland in Dorset when the jib of their Coles crane touched overhead power cables as they salvaged a Heinkel 111 which had crashed there on 25 September 1940. In yet another accident, an airman was crushed to death when an aero engine rolled from the lorry onto which it was being loaded. Wreck recovery was certainly not without its dangers.

It was a busy summer for Arthur Nicholls. On 19 September 1940, he was despatched by 49 MU to inspect a Spitfire that had crashed near Hartfield. His trip provides an excellent example of the difficulties the salvage gangs experienced in the hectic days of the Battle of Britain. The aircraft in question, Spitfire R6971, was being flown by 72 Squadron's Pilot Officer Ernest Edward Males when it was shot down during combat with a force of Messerschmitt Bf 110s. Males had baled out uninjured, leaving his aircraft to plummet to earth, slamming into the ground at Culver's Farm near Hartfield.

'I inspected the site of crash at Culvers Farm,' Nicholls subsequently noted, 'and was informed by the lady owing the farm that the aircraft was removed on Wednesday, September 4th (the same day as it crashed) by a party of Royal

Engineers. The farmer's son had salved from the wreckage a name plate which I inspected and on which was this number: "Type; Spitfire, Serial No.; AP/69/46385".'

'Whilst interrogating the farmer's son I discovered that another Spitfire had crashed near Hartfield. Thinking this may be the one for which we were looking I proceeded with the gang to Swift's Farm, Nr. Withyham, Hartfield. I found there an engine only, No: Merlin 30329, being guarded by the military authorities; I was informed that the fuselage and wings had been taken away by the RAF and they were returning to take away the engine. It would therefore appear that Spitfire R6971 has already been cleared.'

On 2 September 1940, Flying Officer D.B. Bell-Salter flying a 253 Squadron Hurricane Mk.I, serial V6640, was shot down over Rye. He baled out wounded, whilst his aircraft fell to the ground near the town. It was a number of weeks before Arthur Nicholls was requested to undertake a recovery of the fighter. However, sometimes the instructions given to Nicholls were somewhat vague and imprecise, as he was about to discover.

'I ascertained the location of this machine from the Police at Rye,' he wrote, 'as having crashed on the foreshore near the Old Castle ruins immediately in front of the town. This aircraft is completely burnt out, both fuselage and engine. Inspecting the remains I discovered a piece of the fuselage bearing the following number – V6623.'

Nicholls had been directed to the wrong crash site. He had, in fact, come across the wreckage of an 85 Sqaudron Hurricane shot down near Winchelsea on 29 August 1940.

'Amongst the wreckage,' continued Nicholls, 'were burnt pieces of the pilot's uniform from which I salved a piece of the pocket with a linen tab bearing the following – "Gieves Ltd. L/5/38. 40/16207 H.R. Hamilton". I have instructed a gang to clear the wreckage tomorrow, Saturday the 28th inst.'

A Canadian from Oak Point, New Brunswick, 23-year-old Flight Lieutenant Harry Raymond Hamilton was killed in the crash. He was buried with full military honours in Hawkinge Cemetery.

On occasions, the sheer volume of work required the civilian contractors to work together. One example was the events of 27 October 1940, when Arthur Nicholls became involved in the recovery of the remains of a Bf 109 from near the North End Promenade at Littlestone in Kent. The aircraft in question had been shot down on Tuesday, 22 October by Flying Officer Coke of 257 Squadron during a combat over the Channel at about 16.30 hours. The Bf 109 broke up in mid-air, with the bulk of the airframe falling into the sea off Littlestone Golf Links. The pilot, Uffz Arp, was killed.

'Messrs Coast Transport had carried out this clearance and reported that this aircraft had crashed in the sea and that the wreck was not visible any longer, even at low tide. Parts of the fuselage of this machine had been strewn along the Promenade and had been collected by a squad of the 7th Dorsets and taken to their head-quarters on the Promenade. These sections were cleared and it is thought that the small amount of wreckage did not justify a visit to Faygate specially and I have instructed Coast Transport to put it on a lorry when next they are returning a crashed aircraft to Faygate.'

With the daily arrival at 49 MU of wrecked aircraft, British and German, a vast graveyard of jumbled aeroplanes soon formed there. Photographs taken of the yard in 1940 show a huge mountain of assorted wreckage, all of it consigned for eventual re-processing at another vast depot at Banbury, Oxfordshire, by the Northern Aluminium Company. It was to Banbury that most of the wreckage at Faygate was eventually finally taken, along with thousands of aluminium pots, pans, hot-water bottles, tennis racquets, car badges and sundry other items following an appeal to the British public for aluminium.

Not all of the wrecked aircraft were immediately processed for scrap. A number of the more intact German examples were earmarked for technical evaluation or for public display around the country in the various 'Spitfire Fund' drives or for 'War Weapons Week' exhibitions. The task of transporting these aircraft often fell to Nicholls & Co., with the firm's men collecting the requisite Luftwaffe machine and transporting it to the public exhibition site where they would set it up for display and, later on, dismantle the aircraft and return it to Faygate or go on to another venue.

Post-war, the site of 49 MU at Faygate became a timber yard. More recently it has been developed for sheltered residential housing. The site of the Banbury processing depot later became the location of Messrs Bibby's Agricultural Feeds and Seeds plant.

Given the number of aircraft downed across the country during 1940 and 1941 the scale of work carried out by the salvage gangs, both military and civilian, was enormous. That a record is still extant, both photographic and documentary, is largely due to the foresight of the late Arthur Nicholls when he preserved many of his original 1940 documents and photographs.

Preparations for war resulted in an increased number of training-related and other accidents to RAF aircraft. This was the mangled wreckage of Hurricane L1593 of Biggin Hill-based 79 Squadron photographed at Ditchling Common in East Sussex where the aircraft crashed during a thunderstorm on 20 June 1939 whilst on a direction-finding homing flight. The accident resulted in the death of its pilot, Sgt L.F. Davis, RAF (VR), and attracted crowds of curious sight-seers and souvenir hunters. This image also highlights the pending logistical headache for the RAF once war was declared just three months later: how to salvage and recover crashed aircraft? At the time this photograph was taken it was very often simply the case that the motor transport section of the nearest RAF unit, or else the engineering officer of the squadron involved, would simply detail a party to go out and collect the pieces. Clearly, that was neither a sufficient nor a practical solution once war was declared.

(*Above*) Here, both of the Junkers Jumo 211 engines from the dismantled Junkers 88 are taken away by a tractor unit and an RAF flat-bed trailer.

(*Opposite page*) Although the first German aircraft was brought down in the United Kingdom as early as October 1939 it was the Battle of France, throughout the early part of 1940, that first saw the RAF dealing with shot down Luftwaffe aircraft in any numbers. Here, a party of airmen have a Junkers 88 already partially dismantled and ready to transport away at a location 'somewhere in France'. As the battle gathered in intensity under the full weight of the German Blitzkreig, so it became the case that recovering wrecks like this one would no longer be either possible or practicable. Instead, in the retreat to Dunkirk and the Channel coast, enemy and allied aircraft wreckages alike were simply abandoned.

(*Above*) The first enemy aircraft were being downed over the British Isles from October 1939 onwards, but by early 1940 Luftwaffe activity over the country was increasing and gathered in tempo as the Battle of France reached its zenith and culminated in the Dunkirk evacuation. From June 1940 onwards German aircraft losses increased over British soil and the wreckages that resulted all needed to be cleared away. By now, a series of service Maintenance Units had been established across Britain as part of RAF Maintenance Command, all falling under the command of Air Vice Marshal J.S.T. Bradley OBE. It very quickly became apparent that the challenges facing many of the MUs in recovering wrecks, both German and RAF, would be both varied and testing. Here, the remnants of a Heinkel 111 rests in shallow water at Cley-next-the Sea near Blakeney, Norfolk, after being shot down there on the night of 18/19 June 1940. The aircraft, from 4./KG4, had been caught in searchlights and then attacked by an RAF Blenheim which damaged the fuselage and engines. Unable to make a return crossing of the North Sea the pilot ditched offshore and the crew then swam ashore, one of them severely wounded. On board was Major Dietrich Freiherr von Massenbach, the Gruppenkommandeur of II Gruppe KG4, of which the 4./KG4 was part. Illustrative of salvage difficulties that faced the RAF maintenance units, this aircraft was deemed too difficult to recover and was left in situ before being blown up in 1969.

(*Opposite page*) Posing rather less difficulty for the salvage teams this was all that was left of a Heinkel 115 seaplane that crashed and exploded at The Old Rectory, Eyke, Suffolk on 7 June 1940. The aircraft had been on a mine-laying sortie but flew into the ground after the pilot was apparently dazzled by searchlight beams. The mine on board detonated in the crash killing Oblt zur See Adolf von Hullen and Fw Ludwig Fehr. The aircraft was blown to pieces, and here a group of RAF airmen manhandle a section of airframe away from the crash scene. In the second image, one of the seaplane floats can be seen behind the army officer and policeman. What was left was fit only for the scrapheap.

(*Above*) Considerable intelligence value could often be found in even the most shattered and broken-up of wrecks. Here, as an RAF airman picks amongst the fragmented remnants of this Heinkel 111 shot down at Bishop's Court, Chelmsford on 19 June 1940, he finds this Luftwaffe target map. Such discoveries could often give clues as to German operating bases, targets etc. and were useful pieces of intelligence.

(*Opposite page*) One of the earliest enemy aircraft crashes in Kent was this Dornier 17 of 8./KG77 shot down by Hurricanes of 32 Squadron into a hop garden between Beech Farm and Sheephurst Farm at Collier Street near Paddock Wood on 3 July 1940. The aircraft, which drew crowds of sightseers, was a relatively easy recovery job for the salvage party and became one of the first aircraft recovered by 49 MU, RAF Faygate, who dealt with the majority of wartime crashes in Kent, Sussex and Surrey. One of the RAF airmen guarding the wreck crouches to examine the colourful unit emblem beneath the cockpit and, in another pose, points out the many bullet holes that had ripped into the Dornier's fuselage.

The first of many Messerschmitt 109s to be shot down onto British soil during 1940 was this aircraft of 3./LG2 which fell at Buckland Farm, Sandwich, Kent on 8 July. Here, a party from 49 Maintenance Unit, RAF Faygate, make an effort to dig out the wreckage whilst the local constabulary keep watch to keep at bay the souvenir hunters. In truth, a number of Police officers helped themselves to a trophy or two as was evidenced by a number of retired officers revealing their own personal booty in post-war years.

Here the salvage party have dug down to the smashed fin and tail wheel. On the crumpled remnants of the fuselage can be seen the unit emblem: Mickey Mouse carrying an umbrella. They didn't dig much further, as an excavation at the crash site revealed much later.

In the late 1970s the Kent-based Brenzett Aeronautical Museum finished off the work of 49 MU using a mechanical excavator to retrieve this deeply buried and chalk-encrusted DB601 engine. The difficulty in 1940 of extracting engines that were buried like this generally made such salvage jobs impractical. The wrecks were more often than not left buried, surface wreckage cleared, and the impact craters filled.

Another buried Messerschmitt ended up in the middle of the road at Byron Avenue, Margate on 24 July 1940 and it became a case of quickly clearing the wreckage and filling in the crater to get the traffic flowing again. Whilst fire officers and an RAF officer inspect the debris an airman stands guard, bayonet fixed, as other firemen take a ladder to deal with wreckage that has been thrown onto a nearby rooftop. The pilot, Lt Josef Schauff of 8./JG26, fell dead in nearby playing fields with an unopened parachute.

Sometimes, as we have seen in the previous image, falling aircraft didn't always crash harmlessly into fields and countryside. This was the aftermath when a Heinkel 111 of 3./KGr126 was hit and disabled by the Harwich anti-aircraft battery before crashing out of control into houses at Victoria Road, Clacton-on-Sea, killing all four crew members. On board were three 'C' type mines, two of which exploded in the crash. The subsequent fire, which destroyed a number of houses and damaged many more, killed two civilians and injured another 150. In one of these views, RAF technicians are already taking apart the wreckage having dealt with the grisly aftermath of the crash and removed the bodies of the four German airmen. Another aspect of the involvement of the RAF in dealing with such incidents was the service's responsibility to bury deceased Luftwaffe airmen with full military honours and the third image of this series shows the funeral for the four fliers at Clacton with an RAF bearer party and honour guard.

(*Above*) Standard equipment for lifting and removal of aircraft wrecks was the ubiquitous Coles crane. Photographs of work actually underway to remove crashed aircraft are somewhat rare, and those that do exist are often posed. However, here we have an RAF maintenance unit in the throes of loading the smashed wreckage of a Junkers 88 onto a flat-bed truck. In this instance, the wreck is that of a Junkers 88 shot down at Martinhoe Common, Lynton, Devon on 24 July 1940. Sections of the aircraft have already been manhandled into heaps ready for removal, with both propeller assemblies prominent in the foreground.

(*Left*) Sometimes it wasn't that easy! Here the Coles crane from 49 MU, RAF Faygate, has come a cropper in a farm ditch as it attempts to access a crashed aircraft on Romney Marsh, Kent in 1940.

(*Above*) And it wasn't just the transport that sometimes had a hard job. Here, a party from 49 MU drags sections of a crashed aircraft across a Kent hop field. Judging by the empty hop garden and the warm clothing this is either very early in 1940 or much later in the year. The work of the salvage parties was often arduous, cold and dirty; and it certainly wasn't glamorous.

(*Opposite page*) The accommodation, too, for the 49 MU recovery parties could be little more than basic. Temporary billets might be found in nearby households, but often the living quarters would be in barns and outhouses if the salvage job ran over more than one day away from the Faygate area. Usually, though, accommodation was simply under canvas as illustrated here whilst the airmen from RAF Faygate deal with the dismantling and removal of an RAF Lysander at Marshfoot Lane, Hailsham, East Sussex. The aircraft of 16 Squadron, RAF, had become bogged-in during an emergency landing on 13 March 1940 and it was not possible for the Lysander to be flown out due to the ground conditions.

Two of the RAF crash inspectors based at RAF Faygate in 1940 were Pilot Officer Bernard Clarke (right) and Flying Officer Jenkins who are seen here with the unit staff car in Horsham town centre during the summer of 1940 at the height of the Battle of Britain. Their task was to visit each crash site, British and German, decide how the recovery should be tackled and the men and equipment required, and then to issue appropriate orders. Later in the war, 49 Maintenance Unit also had its own Damage Officer who would assess damage to buildings, agricultural land etc occasioned by crashing aircraft or by the subsequent salvage efforts, and he would also make recommendations as to appropriate compensation under the government's war damage scheme.

Frequently, the aircraft dealt with by the recovery teams were somewhat less intact than the Lysander at Hailsham. Here, soldiers pick amongst all that is left of a Junkers 88, shot down at Church Farm, Aylesford on 18 August 1940. The aircraft has been comprehensively smashed to pieces with only the main wing-spar identifiable in this photograph. Crash Inspector Pilot Officer Bernard Clarke was assigned to visit this crash site where he noted: 'Scrap only'. This photograph bears ample testimony to Clarke's blunt assessment.

(*Above*) Another Heinkel 111 that, like the aircraft near Blakeney, had defeated the RAF Maintenance Units was this aircraft of I./KG4 that flew into a mountainside at Eastman's Cairn, Cairnsmore-of-Fleet on 8 August 1940. Whilst RAF personnel and Intelligence Officers managed to reach the wreckage, it proved impossible to get it off the mountain and, in fact, the wreckage remained in situ until at least the 1980s when it was lifted off by helicopter for museum display. Remoteness of wrecks such as this one often meant that they were left where they were, although the RAF went to extraordinary lengths to salvage some wrecks.

(*Opposite page*) Less challenging was the recovery of a Junkers 87 'Stuka' shot down at St Lawrence on the Isle of Wight during an attack on ships of Convoy CW9 '*Peewit*' on 8 August 1940. Here, a salvage party from 49 MU Faygate pose with their trophy before dismantling and transportation gets underway, involving what was actually the first intact Junkers 87 to fall into British hands. Later, the airmen involved pose with the 'Stuka' on its Queen Mary low-loader trailer while they stop for refreshment on their way back across the island to board the Cowes ferry and journeying back to RAF Faygate. Note how the fuselage has been stowed on its side, with the wings neatly stacked alongside. Not only were crashed aircraft attractive to souvenir hunters in situ, but they also attracted them when being transported and had to be guarded against pillaging by a trophy-eager public!

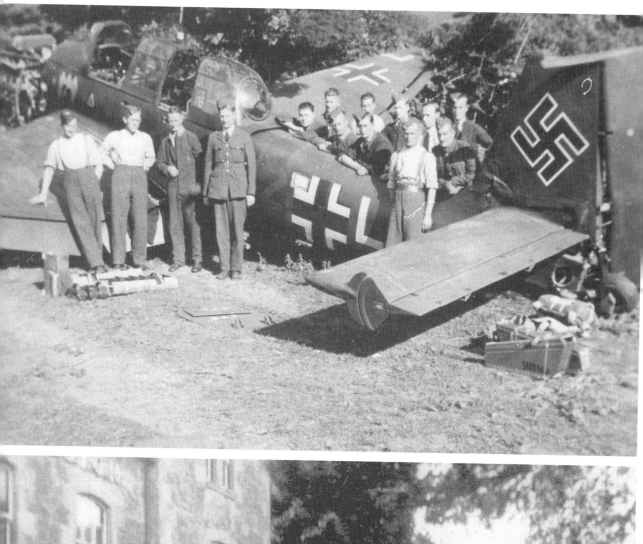

(*Above*) When this Messerschmitt 109 E was shot down into Poole Harbour on 13 August 1940 it was pulled out of the water by local boatmen and brought ashore for display in a sports ground in order to raise funds for the 'Spitfire Fund'. Notable by its absence is the DB 601 engine and propeller, and doubtless these heavy items still remain firmly embedded in the mud of the harbour floor. Parts of this aircraft were being sold off for 6d a piece to further boost funds for the Spitfire appeal, and when the display was concluded the pitiful remnants of the Messerschmitt were collected for 'processing' at RAF Faygate. No doubt the collection party were greatly relieved that, on this occasion, they simply had to collect the mangled remains from a convenient hard-standing with no tedious effort through mud, water, forest or marshland.

(*Opposite above*) A case in point was this Messerschmitt 109 of 6./JG51 that was shot down after combat with RAF Hurricanes and Defiants and ended up on its belly in a field at East Langdon in East Kent after sustaining damage to its oil tank on 24 August, 1940. Its pilot, Ofw Fritz Beeck, was taken into captivity. Here, two Australian soldiers spy out a nice trophy in the form of this colourful fuselage emblem which depicts a weeping pelican with an umbrella under its arm. Beneath are the words 'Gott Strafe England' ('God Punish England').

(*Opposite below*) It didn't take long for the soldiers to have their trophy away, and here is the same aircraft with the emblem cut from both sides of the fuselage. The swastika has also been hacked from the tail fin.

(*Above*) On 16 August 1940 a number of vehicles belonging to 49 MU were destroyed in the Junkers 87 dive-bombing attack against RAF Tangmere and this loss of transport caused problems for the already hard-pressed unit in dealing with an ever increasing tally of crashed aircraft that needed to be dealt with. As the backlog of cases built up, the Air Ministry decided there was no other option than to engage civilian contractors working under the direction of RAF Faygate.

(*Right*) Aircraftsmen Jim Cookson and Bert Whitehead man the defensive gun post at RAF Faygate, with Cookson having acquired a Luftwaffe flare pistol which rests by his foot. He later told how he claimed this was officially to alert personnel at RAF Faygate of an imminent attack, though he later disclosed that it was useless for this purpose because he had fired off all the flare cartridges he could find 'just for fun' and that he regarded the pistol as his own war prize.

The same pair pose on one of 49 MU's surviving pieces of transport after the Tangmere raid. In the background can be seen the RAF Faygate guardroom which was put to post-war use as a site office for Messers Agate & Co., timber merchants.

(*Above*) One of the contractors engaged for service to the RAF were the Brighton-based hauliers, A.V. Nicholls & Co. With their usual peacetime commercial haulage work diminished by hostilities it was inevitable that such companies should be engaged upon war work and proprietor Arthur Nicholls, a one-time Brighton Mayor, embraced his firm's Air Ministry engagement with enthusiasm. Often he would personally visit the crash sites to assess what was required in the way of transport and equipment, and occasionally accompany his gangs as they went about their work. Here (wearing Homburg hat to the left) Arthur Nicholls poses with a lorry and trailer load of wreckage at the 49 MU depot in Faygate. Amongst the items of wreckage can be seen sections of Heinkel 111 wing, Messerschmitt 109 engines, and a float from a Heinkel He 59 seaplane. Piles of aircraft scrap can also be seen off to the right of the lorry bonnet waiting to be processed for scrap and shipped out.

(*Opposite above*) Other haulage firms, too, were enlisted to collect and transport aircraft wreckages. Bizarrely, though, this lorry belonged to the British American Tobacco Company Ltd but has been press-ganged into moving a Heinkel 111 rather than cigarettes. Very much an over-sized load, it will be seen that the main landing wheels are running on the road either side of the lorry bed and almost acting like outrigger stabiliser wheels. A private motor vehicle has been forced to take refuge on the verge while the unusual cargo proceeds down the centre of the carriageway as it heads for its ignominious end at RAF Faygate.

(*Opposite below*) Another Heinkel 111 cargo and yet more civilian trucks. Quite probably these were again the vehicles of A.V. Nicholls & Co., this time moving the wreck of a He 111 that had been shot down on 26 August 1940 at Wick near Littlehampton in West Sussex. One vehicle transports the fuselage while another deals with the engines. Another trailer, not visible in this shot, was used to take away the bulky wings.

(*Above*) The Heinkel 111 on the British American Tobacco Company lorry may well be this one which crash-landed at Westfield Farm, Studland, after sustaining combat damage on 25 September 1940. If so, it hides a tragic story relating to its recovery by a salvage party from 50 Maintenance Unit, Cowley. Two airmen working on the recovery of this aircraft were electrocuted when their Coles crane touched overhead electric cables. The offending power lines can be seen in the background of this photograph. The aircraft, from 1./KG55, carries an impressive white raging bull emblem on its fuselage.

(*Opposite & following*) When Uffz Leo Zaunbrecher crash-landed his battle-damaged Messerschmitt 109 amongst the corn stooks at Lower Mays Farm, Selmeston on 12 August 1940 the fighter had not yet ended its useful life. Its little red devil emblem on the port engine cowling attracted the attention of souvenir hunters and photographers alike. In the second of four photographs, a policeman and a soldier are curious to learn more about the Messerschmitt's cockpit, whilst in the third photograph the Me 109 is pictured at 49 MU, RAF Faygate. In the third image Corporal Robert Anson and LAC James Cookson 'pretend' to remove the emblem from the cowling but, in fact, this is a posed shot and the artwork had already been all but removed during an overnight stop at Lydney, Gloucestershire whilst being taken on an exhibition tour of Cardiff, Birmingham, Manchester, Leeds and Glasgow. In the final image the aeroplane is on public display in Leeds City Square and the half-removed cowling badge can be clearly seen. In this photograph the wings have been re-assembled back to front. The posse of policemen were no doubt present to ensure that no further trophy hunting took place.

(*Above*) Another Messerschmitt 109, also shot down on 12 August 1940, was this aircraft flown by Oblt Albrecht Dresz of III./JG54 which made a good forced-landing at Hengrove, near Margate in Kent. Like the example displayed at Leeds, this Messerschmitt was also placed on public display to raise money for the Spitfire Fund but it is shown here being loaded onto a trailer by the men of 49 MU before being transported to Faygate. Whilst the Me 109 became quite familiar to the inhabitants of South East England its range wouldn't take it much beyond London, and thus the arrival of a bullet-holed Me 109 for exhibition in more northern towns tended to generate a good deal of excitement.

(*Opposite page*) A little less intact was the Messerschmitt 109 of Lt Hans-Herbert Landry of Stab.I/JG3 who was shot down over Whitfield, near Dover on 28 August 1940. Landry descended by parachute, badly injured, and died in hospital from his injuries on 23 September 1940. There was rather less of the aircraft to collect than there was, for example, of Uffz Leo Zaunbrecher's Me 109, but the crash provided an excellent photo opportunity as firemen and soldiers dealt with the burning wreckage by shovelling soil over the smouldering engine. The photographer couldn't resist 'posing' a fireman with his raised pick-axe as he almost symbolically brought it smashing down on the wreckage. The demise of this particular fighter was witnessed by Prime Minister Winston Churchill from Dover Castle and he was later driven to the crash scene to see for himself the handiwork of the RAF fighters. Wrecks such as these generally offered very little in the way of intelligence value and could really not be put to use in the same manner as the aircraft displayed in Leeds, for example. Instead, the scrap yard at 49 MU's Faygate depot would be the staging point before the wreckage was consigned to the Northern Aluminium Company at Banbury, Oxfordshire, for smelting into ingots and subsequently feeding into the British aviation industry as raw material.

And this is some of that 'raw material'. Here, at 49 Maintenance Unit, RAF Faygate, wrecked aircraft, both British and German, were taken for further breaking prior to dispersal for scrap processing. Materials needed to be separated before that process could begin; aluminium alloys, magnesium alloys, steel, copper, brass, plastics and rubber all needed to be sorted and dealt with. Sometimes, further objects of intelligence value were discovered in the mangled wreckage, and other times spare parts for Luftwaffe machines were scavenged in order to rebuild, maintain or return to flight captured German aircraft types that were being evaluated at the Royal Aircraft Establishment, Farnborough. Rather more grisly finds could also made amongst the assorted wreckage and those who worked at Faygate recalled the sometimes unpleasant odour that pervaded the heaps of mangled aircraft parts.

Little wonder, given the scale of aircraft breaking that once went on here, that when the author visited the site of 49 MU at Faygate during 1979 there was still plenty of evidence scattered around of the processing that had taken place on this spot. During the late 1970s and early 1980s the site was a timber yard, and aircraft fragments like these were still strewn far and wide around what had once been RAF Faygate.

(*Right*) It would have been assorted fragments like these that were melted down to be used in these cast alloy 'Victory Bells' that were sold to aid the RAF Benevolent Fund. The bells were designed by Conrad A. Parlanti who was responsible for the large eagle which crowns the RAF Memorial on the Victoria Embankment, and they were initially sold shortly after VE Day. The inscription around the base reads: 'Cast from metal recovered from German aircraft shot down over Britain'.

(*Below*) Whilst the newspaper and magazine publishers of the day tended to favour photographs of shot down wrecks at the places they had come to earth, there was clearly some attraction in illustrating the vast dumps of wrecked aircraft that were being assembled. This was a double-page spread from a news magazine published during the summer of 1940, its origin given away by the page creases! Illustrated here are parts of Messerschmitt 109s and 110s, and a Dornier 17 fuselage section.

CKED GERMAN RAIDERS BROUGHT DOWN
HE R.A.F. AND ANTI-AIRCRAFT GUNNERS.
NG SCRAP METAL FROM THE PLANES

(*Above*) At the Banbury processing plant, workers carry a section of the Dornier 17 fuselage brought from the crash site at Paddock Wood on 3 July 1940 (see page 19). A mass of other enemy aircraft wreckages await the smelter.

(*Opposite page*) Such was the volume of aircraft being shot down in the East Kent area that a temporary 'holding' depot was established at Elham in Kent where assorted wreckages of locally-crashed aircraft were assembled prior to removal to RAF Faygate before further processing and despatch to the Northern Aluminium Company depot at Banbury. The Messerschmitt 109 seen in this image is the aircraft brought down at East Langdon on 24 August 1940 as featured on page 31. Note the holes in the fuselage where the emblems have been hacked out.

(*Above*) In this photograph the Station Commander of RAF Biggin Hill, Group Captain Grice, and the Station Adjutant, Flying Officer Haskell, set about their own spot of souvenir hunting as they remove trophies from the Dornier 17 shot down at Leaves Green, Kent, on 18 August 1940.

(*Opposite above*) Another view of the Banbury plant, with at least three fuselages of Dornier 17s, side by side, and with the hulk of a Junkers 87 'Stuka' in the background. Once non-alloy parts had been stripped out, along with glass, plastics and steel, etc., the alloy remnants were melted down and turned into ingots as raw material for the aviation industry. Not so much as swords into ploughshares as swords into new swords!

(*Opposite below*) Almost certainly this image was also captured at the Banbury plant or a local out-station and shows the Messerschmitt 109 of 3./LG2 shot down at Shellness on 15 September 1940 with its pilot, Uffz August Klick, taken POW. Here it is seen adorned with anti-German graffiti and appears to be in the process of being stripped of souvenirs, judging by the pile of items heaped up on the ground behind the rudder. In the background can be seen the remains of Dornier 17s and a single Junkers 87 'Stuka' against the far fence.

One particular Junkers 87 'Stuka' that was never intended for smelting at Banbury was this example which made a landing with minimal damage on Ham Manor Golf Course near Rustington on 18 August 1940. Such was its condition that it was deemed repairable on-site and was scheduled to be flown out by an RAF test pilot to the Royal Aircraft Establishment at Farnborough. However, and notwithstanding this impressive Home Guard turn-out, the aircraft was literally torn apart by trophy hunters.

Here is all that was left after the souvenir scavengers had finished their destructive work! The locals had ensured that the RAF wouldn't be getting their first flyable Junkers 87 'Stuka'.

Of this Stuka there was precious little left to salvage even before any souvenir hunters got to work. This was the smashed up wreckage of a Junkers 87 that had crashed into houses at Shorncliffe Crescent, Folkestone on 15 August 1940 after being pursued by a Hurricane that sent it careering through the high tension power lines in the background. In the far distance a group of Hurricanes can be seen – most probably returning to their home airfield at nearby RAF Hawkinge.

The raiding of German aircraft wrecks took on a rather different angle when this Dornier 17-Z was shot down near Manor Farm at Stodmarsh in Kent on 13 August 1940. After the crew had been marched off into captivity, Mr Burt of Manor Farm drained the fuel tanks for use in his Albion lorry, apparently aided and abetted by the Army! This is Mr Burt looking suitably pleased with himself after his unexpected aerial fuel delivery as he is photographed with the Dornier and his equally smug soldier 'assistants'.

(*Above*) On the same day, yet another Dornier 17-Z was shot down over Barham in Kent and ended up crashing onto the railway line there. There was a pressing need to re-open and keep 'permanent' the Permanent Way, and here wreckage is piled up against the Pherbec railway bridge as the village policeman mounts guard.

(*Opposite above*) Here, a civilian salvage gang employee looks particularly pleased with himself as he prepares to set about the wrecked fuselage with a rather substantial crow bar. Bullet strikes are plainly visible in this photograph.

(*Opposite below*) The majority of aircraft illustrated in this book depict Luftwaffe types and this perhaps presents a distorted image of the nationalities of the machines being brought down. Of course, British aircraft were being lost in large numbers too, but photography of such crashes for publication would not have passed the press censorship bureau. Clearly, photographs of shot down British aircraft would not have been good for morale and therefore such photographs are rare. Private photography was strictly limited by The Control of Photography Order, and even if photographs were sneakily taken by civilians then they risked prosecution if placing them for development and printing through conventional sources. Added to that, there were very significant difficulties in acquiring film, and developing and printing materials, during the war years. Here, however, is a considerable rarity; a photograph of a downed RAF Hurricane during the Battle of Britain. This was the aircraft flown by Sgt 'Jim' Hallowes of 43 Squadron from RAF Tangmere who made a forced-landing at Amberley, West Sussex, when he experienced engine problems during a patrol on 20 July 1940. The aircraft was collected by 49 MU, taken to a civilian repair organisation depot, and later returned to operational service.

(*Above*) The RAF Maintenance Units were also responsible for removing aircraft that had crashed or otherwise come to grief on RAF airfields. This included this Hurricane of 615 Squadron, badly damaged by bomb blast at RAF Kenley following an air raid on 18 August 1940.

(*Opposite page*) The pilot of this Hurricane was not so lucky. In this incident, another Tangmere based pilot, Flt Lt Carl Davis of 601 Squadron, was killed when his aircraft was shot down and crashed into the garden of Canterbury Cottage at Matfield in Kent. Curious locals came to view the wreck and were charged 6d by the owner of the cottage to gain access to the garden, with all proceeds going to the Spitfire Fund. The villager on the right looks intent on getting his six-pennyworth, as he appears to be helping himself to something in the starboard wing gun-bay. By the time 49 MU arrived to take away the wreck it had been quite extensively plundered by souvenir hunters. On the plus side, though, several pounds had been raised for a new Spitfire.

(*Above*) Again at Kenley, this Miles Magister light communications aircraft was completely wrecked in a bombed and collapsed hangar on the same day. Of largely wood and fabric construction there would have been little of any scrap value here. However, RAF maintenance units would have stripped all usable parts such as instruments, propellors, engines, wheels etc., from wrecks like this. If it could be salvaged, then as far as was reasonably possible nothing was wasted.

(*Opposite above*) Another civilian lorry is pressed into use to collect and remove the wreckage of a Messerschmitt 110 shot down at Honeysuckle Lane, High Salvington, near Worthing on 4 September 1940 as the recovery gang give a cheery thumbs-up. The three scaffold tubes would have been used to make a tripod for a block-and-tackle in lieu of a Coles crane in order to lift the sections of airframe onto the lorry. Mudguards and other vehicle extremities were painted white to better aid visibility in the blackout.

(*Opposite below*) There would have been little need for either Coles crane or tripod to remove these sections of Messerschmitt 110 that comprised the wreckage of the aircraft of Erprobungsgruppe 210 shot down at Broadbridge Farm, Horley, Surrey on 15 August 1940. Scattered wreckage has been heaped into this pile ready for collection and would have been light enough to manhandle onto a truck. Meanwhile, a soldier stands guard with his anti-aircraft Bren gun.

(*Above*) An unidentified Junkers 88 at an unidentified location is daubed with a 'V for Victory' emblem and the corresponding Morse code symbols for the letter 'V'. This looks to be another example of civilian gangs removing wrecked aircraft and may well show employees of A.V. Nicholls & Co. Ltd at work, perhaps taking heaped and assorted wreckages from RAF Faygate to Banbury.

(*Opposite above*) This Junkers 88, with its broken back, was shot down on 9 September 1940 at Newells Farm, Nuthurst, West Sussex, where it had been substantially 'got at' by souvenir hunters when this photograph was taken. The trampled soil around the wreck tells its own story of multiple visitors. Although the swastikas have been stripped from the tail the culprit was apprehended and required to leave his prize trophies leaning against the wreck to the left of this photograph. Although this trophy hunter didn't get away with it, plenty of others did. A great many relics were taken from crashed aircraft like this and more than seventy years later still keep turning up. Although it was illegal at the time, many of these items are now of great interest and value to researchers, historians, museums and private collectors.

(*Opposite below*) More wreckage for Banbury was collected by A.V. Nicholls & Co. from the grounds of The Gordon Boys Home at Chobham, Surrey where this Heinkel 111 of 6./KG26 had been shot down by anti-aircraft fire on the night of 23/24 September 1940. All of the crew had baled out, and so this burnt and shredded parachute must have been a spare that was on board the bomber. Of the wreckage, most was burnt and scattered over a wide area, although salvage gang member Bob Sawyers still managed to set fire to surrounding grass land as he cut up the larger pieces of Heinkel.

(*Above*) A Royal Navy Reserve Lieutenant from The Thames Patrol paddles in the mud to inspect what is left of a Spitfire shot down off Hoo Marina in the Thames Estuary on 5 September 1940. This would certainly have been a challenging job for the Maintenance Unit gangs, being located in deep tidal mud. Nevertheless, much of this wreckage was ultimately removed although the heavier parts were not retrieved until the 1980s when they were salvaged by a team of enthusiasts. The pilot of this Spitfire, Flying Officer P.J.C. King of 66 Squadron, baled out but unfortunately he was killed when his parachute failed to open.

(*Opposite above*) Dismantling of this Dornier 17 of 8./KG76, shot down at Castle Farm, Shoreham, Kent, is already well underway after being downed on Sunday 15 September 1940 – 'Battle of Britain Day'. Stripped panels have been heaped in the foreground as a trailer stands ready to the left of the starboard wing and the salvage crew continue their work. In this instance, the gang seems to include civilians, RAF personnel and soldiers.

(*Opposite below*) Another 'Battle of Britain Day' casualty was also this Dornier 17 that crashed onto the forecourt of Victoria Station following a mid-air collision with an RAF Hurricane over central London. In the crash, the shop of well-known clock supplier James Walker Ltd was badly damaged and a mass of mantel clocks are scattered across the pavement.

(*Above*) Although the bulk of the mangled wreckage at Victoria Station posed little difficulty for access by the salvage gangs, the severed tail section that landed on a nearby rooftop was probably a little more challenging to remove. This was arguably the most photographed and most famous German aircraft loss in the whole of the Battle of Britain, occurring as it did in central London and on what is universally celebrated as Battle of Britain Day.

(*Opposite page*) 'Your chimney swept, madam?' This was the aftermath of yet another German aircraft that struck another building after being shot down. This incident was at Maidstone in Kent on 5 September 1940 with a Messerschmitt 109 crashing into a house at 6 Hardy Street. Ironically, the emblem for this Me 109 unit (I./JG54) depicted a chimney sweep with his ladder and in this instance the soot certainly seems to have been comprehensively cleared from this particular chimney. Note the impact mark of a wing across the tiled roof. Only the tail section is recognisable, and lies in a smouldering heap in the back garden leaving little for the salvage parties from 49 MU to actually collect. Uffz Fritz Hotzelmann, the pilot, had baled out at very low level to land on a roof in John Street before being taken POW. Despite its extensive damage the house was repaired and is still standing.

(*Above*) Whilst the Victoria Station Dornier 17 crash was very widely photographed, little attention was paid to the wrecked Hurricane that fell in the roadway nearby at the junction of Ebury Bridge Road with Buckingham Palace Road. Here, however, we see a pile of wreckage that has been collected from the highway and placed against an adjacent wall to await collection. The priority was in getting London traffic moving once again, and the crater that contained the Rolls Royce Merlin engine and other wreckage was simply filled in and covered over. In 2004 the engine was recovered during a televised archaeological 'dig' in the presence of its former pilot, Sgt Ray Holmes, from 504 Squadron, who had baled out of the aircraft after colliding with the Dornier.

(*Opposite above*) With aerial battles going on above a highly populated region it was inevitable that crashing aircraft would sometimes end up striking buildings, and this is another example. Looking more like a bombed building than an aircraft crash site this is, in fact, the scene at Richmond Avenue, Merton, after a Junkers 88 bomber had crashed into a pair of residential dwellings on the night of 19/20 September 1940. One civilian, 25-year-old Mary Butcher, died from her injuries and three of the four crew were killed in the crash whilst the fourth crew member baled out into captivity. Salvage workers pick amongst the ruins, but all that seems to be left of the twin-engine bomber is a ball of mangled airframe wreckage that can be seen on the rubble in the top left of the photograph. Unlike the incident in Hardy Street these houses were clearly beyond any repair, and new dwellings were subsequently built on the site.

(*Opposite below*) And yet another German aircraft that came to grief in a residential area. This time, just the tail section and a portion of wing spar seems to be about all that is left for 49 MU to collect after a Heinkel 111 of Stab III./KG1 smashed itself to pieces amongst the bungalows and houses of Manor Avenue, Caterham on the night of 26/ 27 August 1940. Having suffered a direct hit from anti-aircraft fire during a night mission to bomb factories in the Coventry area, the crew ditched their bombs and then all baled out into captivity. Four days later the burned out wreckage was collected and taken away to RAF Faygate.

(*Above*) A few days later, and not too far away from Caterham, another Heinkel came to grief but this time in a mid-air collision with a Hurricane of 79 Squadron on 30 August 1940. This is all that remained of the Hurricane after Plt Off E.J. 'Teddy' Morris had baled out. Meanwhile, a herd of unconcerned cows graze around the still smouldering wreckage at Lodge Farm, South Holmwood, Surrey. The charred and twisted wreckage ended up being thrown onto the same trucks as the jumbled remains of the Caterham Heinkel. The 49 MU salvage party passed through South Holmwood, with the intermingled debris of both aircraft going back into the wartime re-cycling and salvage effort.

(*Opposite page*) Another Messerschmitt 109 shot down in a residential area during the Battle of Britain was this aircraft of 6./JG52 that crashed on 20 October 1940 in the middle of a group of temporary houses for bombed-out Londoners. Luckily, none of the flimsy wooden dwellings were hit by the crashing fighter and the demise of this Me 109 ended up being a morale boosting event for the war weary residents. Here, a soldier mounts sentry duty on what seems to be a grey rainy day. An RAF Corporal, in charge of the salvage party from RAF Faygate, makes a quick assessment as to the methodology for the removal of this aircraft at Wickham Street, Welling. The close proximity of buildings meant that it probably had to be hauled out by manpower and winches, rather than by Coles crane.

(*Opposite page & above*) Another inverted Messerschmitt and another job for 49 MU's Coles crane came on 30 September 1940 in Windsor Great Park when a Messerschmitt 109 of 7./JG27 made a forced-landing there after being damaged by fighters during a bomber escort mission to London. In executing the emergency landing, Oblt Karl Fischer's Me 109 turned over onto its back although, miraculously, Fischer was captured unhurt after what could easily have been a fatal crash. For the MU salvage party it was first a case of righting the enemy fighter before preparing it for removal.

Righted by the Coles crane, the Messerschmitt 109 is subject to eager attention by the RAF salvage gang. One group are intent on the wing gun and its ammunition while another party seem more interested in what they can find in the cockpit.

(*Opposite page*) Given that Fischer's Messerschmitt had landed in the King's back garden it seems only appropriate that it should have later been exhibited in His Majesty's front yard! On 3 October 1940 the Messerschmitt was displayed to raise money for the Royal Borough of Windsor's Spitfire Fund and during that time the German fighter was visited by the Princesses Elizabeth and Margaret, with Princess Elizabeth being allowed to sit in the pilot's seat. This later gave rise to one wag at 49 MU, RAF Faygate, asking if his unit could now display a 'By Royal Appointment' coat of arms.

(*Above*) The removal of souvenirs or trophies from crash sites, German or British, was strictly forbidden. Indeed a number of prosecutions took place of persons accused of taking such items, although this did very little to dissuade others from the practice. Sometimes the souvenir had little more than curiosity 'value' although some trophies had a rather more practical value. Here, the tail wheel from the Heinkel 111 shot down at Hale on 29 August was put to good use on a wheelbarrow having been squirrelled away from the crash scene before the RAF Maintenance Unit arrived.

(*Opposite above*) An unusual breakdown job! With no Coles crane, this salvage party have pressed into service a breakdown truck from a local garage in order to lift the Messerschmitt 109 of Uffz Hamer who put his Me 109 down close to the cricket pavilion at Pelsham House, Peasmarsh on 30 September 1940. The wings have been removed and loaded, and wooden sleepers are being placed under the fuselage and engine to gradually raise the aircraft level with a flat-bed truck or trailer. More often than not, improvisation was the order of the day when collecting these wrecked aircraft.

(*Opposite below*) Crashing Heinkel 111s seemed to have a particular affinity for houses, this one ending up in the back garden of a house at Hale near Fordingbridge in Hampshire on the night of 29/30 August 1940, having been shot down by a Spitfire of 92 Squadron flown by Plt Off A.R. Wright. The crew all baled out, but one of them subsequently succumbed to his injuries.

(*Above*) Sometimes even substantially intact aeroplanes like this Heinkel 111 of KG55, shot down onto the beach at East Wittering, West Sussex on 26 August 1940, defied all attempts at recovery. Just yards from the foreshore, this aircraft would literally sink into the sands as successive tides came and went and the relentless action of the English Channel subsequently broke up and dispersed the protruding remains. Many years later, during the 1970s, some of the remaining wreckage was dug out of the beach by enthusiasts.

(*Opposite page*) Digging out the buried wreckages of aircraft was done with varying degrees of enthusiasm by the MU salvage parties and very often depended upon site accessibility, depth of the buried aircraft, availability of equipment and manpower. An additional factor might well have been the need to retrieve the remains of any aircrew still trapped in the wreckage – such assignments obviously being extremely unpopular with the salvage parties. In this instance, a Messerschmitt 109 of II./JG54 has been shot down close to RAF Biggin Hill at Layhams Farm on 30 August 1940. Despite its accessibility from a nearby road, and the closeness to the RAF station, only the shattered pieces of surface wreckage were cleared away, leaving the engine and fuselage embedded deep in the ground. Squadron Leader John Ellis, CO of the Spitfire-equipped 610 Squadron at RAF Biggin Hill, scowls at the camera as he picks amongst the debris for his personal trophy.

Although this is thought to have been taken at some time after the Battle of Britain it is a good illustration of the efforts sometimes gone to by RAF Maintenance Units in digging out wreckages. Here a party dig out a buried Hurricane, but their undoubted diligence with this particular task might well be influenced by the presence of officers and an official cameraman!

(*Above*) More digging by the men of a 49 MU salvage party. Quite what they are digging out, and where, is a mystery but their Queen Mary lorry and trailer wait in the adjacent lane for another load of aircraft scrap and consignment back to their West Sussex base at Faygate.

(*Left*) And still they dig! Another mystery photograph as an RAF maintenance unit salvage party pose in the crater made by a crashing aircraft during 1940 at an unknown location in the south of England. In this instance, and despite the poor quality of the photograph, the crash seems to have involved a Hurricane, judging from the smashed fragments. The only recognisable item is the butt of a Browning .303 machine that has become embedded vertically in the soil by the force of the impact.

(*Above*) Another job where there were just pieces to pick up was after the shooting down of a Messerschmitt 110 of V./(Z)LG1 at Horam, East Sussex on 27 September 1940. The lads of 49 MU strike a cheery pose with the remnants of this Luftwaffe loss before it joins the ever growing dump at RAF Faygate.

(*Opposite above*) Rather more substantially intact was this Messerschmitt 109 of 3./JG52 which had been shot down at Penshurst Aerodrome, Kent on 27 October 1940. Its pilot, Fw Shieverhofer, was taken prisoner – allegedly by the Spitfire pilot of 74 Squadron who had shot him down and who immediately put down on the Penshurst landing ground to ensure the Luftwaffe pilot's capture. As a rather precariously overhanging load, counterbalanced by its heavy DB 601 engine, the aircraft becomes another consignment for the vehicles of A.V. Nicholls & Co. as it heads out across the Sussex countryside to RAF Faygate on its final journey.

(*Opposite below*) Another oversized load and another Messerschmitt cargo for A.V. Nicholls. This time, the heavy end has been balanced on an improvised extension platform as two New Zealand soldiers ride with the captured Messerschmitt. The aircraft was piloted by Fw Verlings of 1./JG52 and had been shot down on 2 September 1940. Here, it is being taken away from where it had crashed on Tile Lodge Farm, Westbere, near Canterbury.

(*Above*) And another way to transport a Messerschmitt 109! This is the Messerschmitt 109 of Ofw J. Harmeling from 4./LG2 that was shot down at Langenhoe Wick in Essex on 29 October 1940, although this photograph was taken at Victoria Park, Arbroath during 1941 whilst being used for a Spitfire Fund Raising tour of Scotland which included appearances at Glasgow, Stonehaven and Laurencekirk. Once again, souvenir hunters have hacked out the unit emblem from the engine cowling. In this case, the depiction of a Mickey Mouse in black and white and painted on a blue disc has proved irresistible to the tenacious army of trophy hunters who would systematically strip anything they could get their hands on.

(*Opposite above*) Continuing with the theme, this Messerschmitt 109 of 2./JG27 was photographed on an RAF Maintenance Unit Queen Mary low-loader in London during October 1940 outside offices at 161 Clapham Road belonging to another civilian contractor engaged by the Air Ministry for the recovery of aircraft wrecks, Portsmouth Carriers Ltd. The Messerschmitt was left in situ for about a month where it was used as a collecting point for an RAF charity. The writer of the original wartime captions found himself confused by what are clouds of lorry exhaust gasses and ended up describing this as a still-smoking Messerschmitt that had just crashed in a London street. In fact, it had been shot down at The Homestead in the village of Isfield, East Sussex on Sunday 15 September with its pilot, Uffz Andreas Walburger, captured unharmed. The aircraft was later exhibited at a number of other locations in aid of local Spitfire Funds.

(*Opposite below*) The Royal Engineers lend a hand, helping with a gantry and block-and-tackle as they lift the Messerschmitt 109 flown by Oblt Egon Troha of 9./JG3 who made a forced-landing with a damaged radiator at Westcourt Farm, Sheperdswell, Kent on 29 October 1940. The name 'Erika' is painted on the engine cowling above the emblem of the Nordic axe.

(*Above*) A little more care needed to be taken with the recovery of this Hurricane that had made an emergency landing near Folkestone on 7 October 1940. Pilot Officer Ken McKenzie of 501 Squadron had rammed a Messerschmitt 109 in combat over the English Channel, striking the tail of the enemy with his starboard wing tip. Very gingerly McKenzie flew his Hurricane, minus its outboard wing, back to land and executed a safe belly landing. Dismantled, the aircraft was transported to a repair depot and Hurricane V6799 duly returned to service life which it survived until being struck off RAF charge on 9 November 1944. Here is a case in point where the recovery of aircraft by units like 49 MU served a far greater purpose than simply the clearing away of scrap metal.

(*Opposite page*) Here was another job for the MU gangs, and yet another Messerschmitt 109. This time, Gefreiter Bogasch's aircraft is recovered from Northbourne Park near Sandwich after being shot down there on 27 September 1940. It is being lifted with the help of a Royal Engineer party and a lorry-mounted gantry crane, although the recovery party seem singularly disinterested by the task in hand. Perhaps their demeanour is because, by this date during the Battle of Britain and in this locality, such events as crashing German aircraft had become more than commonplace.

(*Above*) Transporting away aircraft like Hurricane V6799 was generally carried out using the RAF Maintenance Unit Queen Mary trailers like these. Here, a damaged Hurricane and a Spitfire are removed for either repair or spares recovery.

(*Opposite above*) When this Junkers 88 of KG51 made a forced landing, out of fuel, at Buckholt Farm near Sidley in East Sussex on 28 July 1940 it was immediately apparent to the RAF that the aircraft was repairable to the standard of flying condition. Given that no flying examples had yet been secured by the RAF for evaluation purposes it was decided to carefully dismantle the aircraft and convey it to the Royal Aircraft Establishment, Farnborough for test flying. Here, some locally based soldiers point out one of the bullet holes they placed in the Junkers as it came into land – the soldiers wrongly believing that they had been responsible for its demise. The aircraft is already being readied for lifting and removal, as witnessed by the wooden blocks.

(*Opposite below*) And this is the very same Junkers 88, but under entirely new management. Repaired, re-painted in British camouflage, and given an RAF serial number the bomber was test-flown by the RAF who were able to glean extremely useful operational and handling data from such evaluation work.

(*Above*) Making an aircraft safe after it had come to grief was an important aspect of the work undertaken by RAF MUs as they dealt with the various crashes. The removal of armaments and ammunition was crucial. Not only were munitions attractive souvenirs to some, but undamaged British ammunition could be put back into the RAF system and used. Here an RAF airman removes belted .303 ammunition from the wing ammunition boxes of a crash-landed Hurricane.

(*Opposite above*) More ammunition. This time an RAF airman and a Royal Artillery soldier examine belted 7.92mm rounds in the wreckage of a Messerschmitt 109 shot down at Chelsham, near RAF Biggin Hill on 30 August 1940. Bullets were popular although dangerous souvenirs, and became valuable 'currency' to schoolboy collectors. The fact that bullets or cannon shells were live and dangerous mattered little to collectors.

(*Opposite below*) There was hardly anything left here, let alone bullets, for anybody to pick up. Looking more like a bomb crater, this was where a Messerschmitt 109 impacted into a drainage ditch on Brede Marshes at Guestling in East Sussex on 25 October 1940 after its pilot had baled out injured and into captivity. Such was the force of the impact in the soft ground that the aircraft has almost entirely disappeared. All that is left for 49 MU to collect can be seen in the background. The rest of the Messerschmitt, engine, fuselage and wing structure, was driven over ten metres into the ground from where it was finally salvaged in the 1980s. Little wonder that the RAF left it where it was in 1940. It would have been quite impractical to salvage it in 1940 given the equipment and resources then available, and it was a more than challenging task for the well-equipped recovery teams several decades later.

In considering the recovery of aircraft in Britain during 1940 it is appropriate to look at similar work being carried out across the other side of the English Channel by the Luftwaffe. Here, units of the Bergungskommando (Salvage Detachments) carried out exactly the same kind of work. Here, and using sheer-legs, they haul a shot down Spitfire off a French beach.

Probably taken early in 1941, here was another Spitfire shot down over France that needed to be dealt with by the Luftwaffe Bergungskommando. Already one of their trucks has arrived at the crash scene.

As in Britain, wrecked aircraft were routinely sent for scrap processing at German depots and here a Luftwaffe airman poses with an RAF Fairey Battle light bomber which has been loaded onto a flat-bed rail truck for transportation to the breakers yard and eventual smelting.

As we have already seen, a considerable number of Messerschmitt 109s were recovered from their various crash sites in a relatively undamaged state and were quickly earmarked for public display at venues the length of the country. Mostly this was in aid of the Spitfire Fund. 49 MU at Faygate, at the heart of the collection of wrecks from Kent and Sussex, were ideally placed to source Me 109s for display purposes. Specimens that were largely intact were generally chosen and were thus spared immediate processing for scrap. Very often one particular airframe would be selected and was then taken on 'tour' before finally being consigned as scrap with its service complete. Here the Me 109 that had been flown by Oblt Gunther Bode of Stab.I/JG27 when he was shot down at Knowle Farm, Mayfield, East Sussex, makes its debut public appearance at Stanhay's Garage in Ashford, Kent.

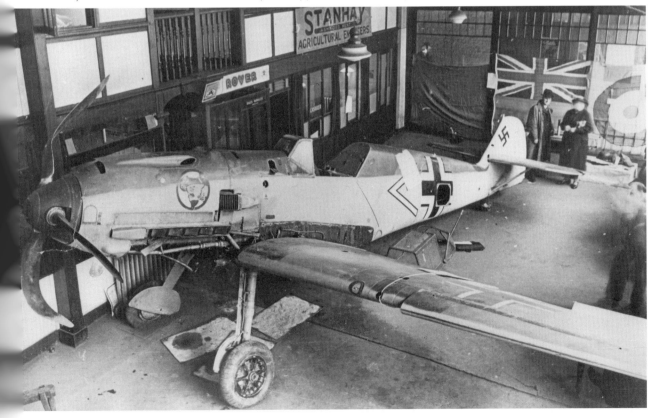

(*Above*) Continuing with that theme, this is the Messerschmitt 109 that ended up on its back in Windsor Great Park (see page 66–69) that was being regularly taken around the country by gangs from 49 MU at Faygate. Here, it is shown whilst on display at Fareham in Hampshire on 14 December 1940. The camouflage netting is intended to hide the Messerschmitt from other enemy aircraft and potential attack and destruction. From Fareham it was eventually collected by A.V. Nicholls & Co. and transported to the Chief Fire Officer at Lyndhurst for a further exhibition there before, time expired, it would finally meet its end in the Banbury smelters.

(*Opposite above*) The Messerschmitt 109 was generally not seen in the air as far west as Truro where this example was exhibited during January and February of 1941. The aircraft had been shot down in Kent at Blean, near Canterbury on 6 September 1940 with its pilot, Uffz Ernst Nittmann, captured unhurt. Previously the aircraft had been displayed at Broad Quay, Bristol, and is thought to have been taken from Truro to Falmouth Docks where it was dismantled and crated ready for shipment to Australia where it was to be further used for display and RAAF recruitment purposes. However the ship on which it was being transported was ultimately sunk and the Messerschmitt never reached its intended destination.

(*Opposite below*) Tunbridge Wells, however, was very much at the heart of 'Messerschmitt country' and the Me 109 was hardly a stranger to most of the locals. An opportunity to get up-close-and-personal with this particular aircraft was presented to townsfolk when it was exhibited at The Assembly Halls for the benefit of the Spitfire Fund. The aircraft was from 3./JG53 and had been shot down on 17 October 1940 at RAF Manston with its pilot, Oblt Walter Rupp, taken POW. The inevitable gaggle of schoolboys lurks nearby, eager for a much closer look or perhaps a crafty souvenir. The Messerschmitt 109 road-show, with a variety of shot down German aircraft, was a feature of a great many towns and villages the length and breadth of Britain. RAF Maintenance Units, most especially number 49 MU, were kept constantly busy transporting these aircraft around the country.

(*Above*) When Oblt Helmut Rau of 3./JG3 crash-landed his battle damaged Messerschmitt 109 on the foreshore at Shoeburyness after combat with a Spitfire of 603 Squadron on 31 August 1940, it was hauled off the beach and into the depot at the nearby army ranges. Here, it was initially deposited in a yard along with other wrecks including an RAF Blenheim that may be seen in the background of this photograph. It will be noted that this Messerschmitt has been moved intact and, at this stage, without the wings having been removed. Later, during October 1940, the aircraft was exhibited in Bolton and other north-west towns before inevitable scrapping.

(*Opposite page*) This Messerschmitt 109 bellied into a wheat field at Northdown alongside the Margate to Broadstairs railway line on 24 July 1940, and its pilot, Oblt Werner Bartels of Gruppen Stab.III/JG26, thereby delivered a near perfect aeroplane for exhibition purposes by the RAF. On its belly, the Messerschmitt was first lifted by the 49 MU Coles crane and its undercarriage lowered, before the salvage party posed with their 'prize'. To avoid detection from the air, the wing and fuselage crosses have been hastily camouflaged with wheat and a large sheet of hessian. A local AFS fireman, Walter Solly, is recorded as having been prosecuted and fined by magistrates for stealing the pilot's side arm from the cockpit of this Messerschmitt. Later, the aircraft went on an exhibition tour with postcards produced to mark its display in Croydon to raise money for the local Spitfire Fund. These were inscribed: 'Made In Germany – Finished In England!' It doubtless struck a chord with the British public at that time.

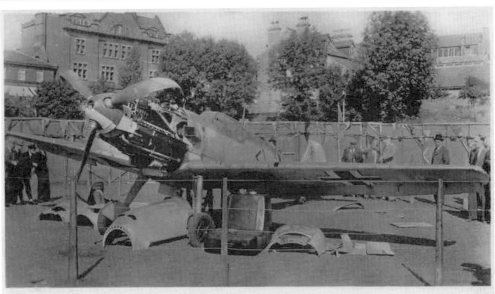

"MADE IN GERMANY — FINISHED IN ENGLAND."
MESSERSCHMITT M.E.109.
C.T. Photo.
ALL PROCEEDS GO TO OUR LOCAL SPITFIRE FUND.

(*Above*) London's Guildhall is the venue here for Gefreiter Herbert Rungen's former mount as his Messerschmitt goes on display to boost the donation of pennies to the Spitfire Fund and here it is being manoeuvred into position by a civilian gang using a heavy crane. Herbert Rungen had made a forced landing at Hastingleigh, near Ashford in Kent on 13 October 1940 after his aircraft was severely damaged in combat with Spitfires. Under the camouflage paint on the fuselage could be discerned the original code letters applied at the factory: B A D Y. Much was made of this, inevitably, for the purposes of some rather childish commentary aimed at morale-boosting at this fund-raising exhibition!

(*Opposite above*) A superb shot of yet more Messerschmitt removals by the men from A.V. Nicholls & Co., this time a long way from home at Barkers Pool, Sheffield, as they prepare another Me 109 for display using the tripod and block-and-tackle arrangement the gangs routinely used for recovery and removal operations. The men had learned by experience the best lifting points and where the centre of gravity was situated on the various aircraft they dealt with. This aircraft had been shot down on 6 September 1940 at Vincents Farm near RAF Manston with Uffz Hans-Georg Schultz captured unharmed. This photograph was taken during October of that year, with 6d being charged for a chance to sit in the cockpit and to be given a photograph of the aircraft – all in aid of the Sheffield Spitfire Fund.

(*Opposite below*) This was a Messerschmitt 109 that was beyond much use as an exhibition piece although, in truth, its crushed, truncated and compressed state would surely have generated a good deal of interest. It is pictured at Spruce Lawns, Elham, Kent on 15 October 1940 after it was said that a bullet from a burst of machine gun fire had detonated its single bomb under the fuselage sending the aircraft down in a shower of pieces and minus its engine and rear fuselage. However the detonation of the bomb by a bullet seems unlikely, and if a 250kg bomb had detonated it is almost certain that the pilot would have been killed instantly and the wreckage far more disintegrated. The centre section has certainly been compressed but, incredibly, Lt Ludwig Lenz was trapped in the cockpit by his legs and found still alive in the wreckage, although he died later that same day in hospital. A group of locally based soldiers are helping themselves to souvenirs against all regulations. A tool kit is in evidence as one soldier chisels the black cross from a wing and the sergeant tries to remove the gun sight from the cockpit.

(*Above*) Even less was left of this Messerschmitt which dived vertically into the South Downs at Falmer, near Brighton on 1 October 1940 and completely disintegrated. No trace was found of its pilot, Uffz Hans Bluder of 4./JG26. Here soldiers scour the fields and pile wreckage in a convenient heap around the smashed engine ready for collection by a 49 MU salvage party. Although right on their doorstep, this seems not to have been a wreck cleared away by the Brighton-based A.V. Nicholls gangers, but the RAF Intelligence Officer noted with some irritation: '… the little wreckage had been removed by the military authorities before arrival of a crash inspector and no details can be given.' Military protocols for dealing with such crashes had clearly been breached, but in truth there would have been very little of any intelligence value to deduce from this shattered wreckage.

(*Opposite above*) Dudley in the West Midlands was the final exhibition venue for this Messerschmitt 109 from the RAF Faygate enemy aircraft 'stable'. The number 13 on the fuselage gave some resonance with its bad luck connotations but in reality its pilot, Oblt Erwin Daig, had been lucky to survive the war as a POW after being shot down at Storrington, West Sussex on 9 September 1940. He could not have thought he was lucky at the time, but the fact of the matter is that had he not been captured his chances of surviving the rest of the war on perhaps the Eastern Front or Home Defence were probably not very high, such was the attrition rate amongst Luftwaffe fighter pilots as the war progressed. Steadily, and as these Messerschmitts were transported around the country, they were gradually depleted of anything removable and portable by rapacious souvenir hunters. Mostly this was by members of the public although those responsible for the transportation and erection of aircraft for display were doubtless equally guilty!

(*Opposite below*) It was souvenir collection at crash sites, though, that presented the greatest challenge to the authorities and here, in a rather desperate measure, the Army have thrown a barbed wire entanglement around a Messerschmitt 109. The aircraft was a machine of 2./JG27 that had made an emergency landing at Harmans Cross in Dorset on 30 November 1940 after a catastrophic engine failure when several pistons and con-rods penetrated the cooling jacket and the engine immediately seized. Uffz Paul Wacker, who was captured unharmed, had been on a weather reconnaissance flight at the time of his mechanical mishap that resulted in over five years of captivity.

(*Above*) This Heinkel 111 is on temporary display in the front car park of The Half Moon pub at Hildenborough in Kent, and only a very short distance from where it was shot down on 11 September 1940. Again a civilian lorry has been pressed into service to take the wreck away, and full advantage is being taken of the public interest aroused by the German bomber as soldiers pass around a collecting tin for the Spitfire Fund. Ironically, and just a little over one month later, a Spitfire crashed vertically into the ground at the back of the pub on 27 October killing its pilot, Plt Off Johnny Mather of 66 Squadron. The same civilian salvage gang who had parked this lorry with its Heinkel cargo in the pub forecourt were back there once again to retrieve what few pathetic shards of Spitfire remained. Once again, and turning tragedy into opportunity, the Spitfire Fund collecting tins were brought out.

(*Opposite above*) Whilst the Messerschmitt 109 was favoured for exhibition purposes because of its size and relative portability, other types were sometimes hauled around the countryside to show to the British public, and this was a Junkers 88 on display at Primrose Hill, London on 10 October 1940. It was an aircraft of 2./KG77 that had been shot down at Gatwick Race Course (now Gatwick Airport) on 27 September 1940 with one of its crew killed and the other three captured but wounded. The sheer size of bomber aircraft often meant that they were displayed as a fuselage only and without their wings.

(*Opposite below*) This Junkers 88, displayed in Wood Green, attracts a curious crowd as the emergency dinghy is exhibited by soldiers. The British public, it seems, never lost their fascination for downed German aircraft that were hauled around the country by RAF Maintenance Units and the Air Ministry's civilian contractors.

(*Above*) From Hildenborough, the same Heinkel was taken on to Mitcham Common in Surrey where it again drew crowds and yet more pennies for the coffers of the Spitfire Fund.

(*Opposite page*) Viewing this exhibited Heinkel 111 at Hayes in Middlesex became an outing for the Douglas family who posed for a family photograph by the tail plane.

(*Above*) Another Junkers 88 put on public display was this aircraft of 8./LG1 which was shot down by Spitfires of 611 Squadron after being sighted over Coventry on 13 November 1940 and eventually crashing at Woodway Farm in Blewbury, Berkshire. This was on the very eve of the infamous Coventry raid. Three of the crew of this Ju 88 were taken prisoner while another had already been killed in the fighter attack. The aircraft was eventually exhibited at St Giles, Oxford, where the Mayor of Oxford, Alderman C.J.V. Bellamy, is seen here inspecting the bomber with two of his fellow councillors. This aeroplane, unlike most others, didn't end up in the Banbury smelters. Instead, the airframe was scheduled for shipment overseas and ended up being exhibited for the Army War Show at Franklin Field, Philadelphia, USA, and at other venues in the States. Its subsequent fate is unknown.

(*Opposite above*) This Junkers 88 was also put on public display, this time as a group of rather self-conscious RAF pilots are 'posed' with the wrecked bomber. The aircraft shown here was from 7./KG30 and had been shot down near Bridlington Reservoir on 15 August 1940 with its four crew captured. It is thought that this photograph was taken not far from the crash site, although some months later.

(*Opposite below*) Another somewhat unusual type for a travelling exhibit in Britain was this Messerschmitt 110 which is photographed being unloaded from its 49 MU Queen Mary low-loader trailer for display at Hendon in North West London, and very close to the current location of the Royal Air Force Museum. It was being exhibited to raise funds for the 'Hendon Four Fighter Fund', a scheme to purchase four Spitfires by local subscription. The aircraft was shot down on 15 August 1940 after a raid on Croydon Aerodrome by the Me 110s of Erprobungsgruppe 210 and had crash-landed at Hawkhurst in Kent. Like the Junkers 88 exhibited in Oxford, this aircraft also found its way to the USA and ended up being shipped to the Northrop Aviation Company for evaluation. Unfortunately, no original genuine Battle of Britain Messerschmitt 110s now exist anywhere in the world, and this aircraft would have made a wonderful exhibit at the future Hendon museum.

(*Right*) As part of the Hendon fund raising scheme, locals were encouraged to buy one penny 'savings stamps' on collecting cards. Once the card was filled in the owner was granted a colourful 'Stamp of Honour' in recognition.

(*Below*) The stark reality of a high speed vertical impact by an out of control aircraft is graphically illustrated here. This was all that was left of a Messerschmitt 110 that had been shot down at Borden, near Sittingbourne, Kent on 9 September 1940. Pretty much all that is left can be seen in this photograph, with the rest of the aircraft having been driven deep underground beneath the crater gouged out by the crash. This was what the salvage parties from 49 MU called a 'Sweep up and leave tidy' job – in other words, take away the surface wreckage and fill in the crater.

This was a Dornier 17 that had been shot down at Wansunt Road, Bexley on 3 November 1940 for what was, by this stage of the Blitz, an increasingly uncommon event: a solo daylight attack by a Luftwaffe bomber aircraft over the British Isles. The target had been Woolwich. The Dornier was intercepted and shot down by Hurricanes of 46 Squadron after being hit by anti-aircraft fire. Still under some control, a forced-landing was attempted on allotments but crashed and broke up after hitting a tree and a brick wall. One of the crew was killed instantly, but the remaining three died in hospital over the following few days. At this recovery task, bombs were dropped across the site overnight whilst the gang from A.V. Nicholls & Co. were off site. One of the Bramo-Fafnir engines from the bomber was lifted bodily by a bomb blast and thrown onto the Nicholls lorry, completely crushing the cab.

49 Maintenance Unit,Faygate. ENEMY AIRCRAFT COLLECTION ORDER. Date. 4/11/40.........

CSO/FAY/10953.

Messrs.H.V.Nichols. District Transport Office.
Princes House. North Street. BRIGHTON.

Please arrange to collect immediately and dispose of aircraft as follows:-

PE & DESCRIPTION. DO.17.   M.U's SERIAL NO.269.

CATION.   Sumpt Road. Bexley.Kent.   CATEGORY. E.

SPOSAL INSTRUCTIONS: to FAYGATE.

        N.B. This order cancels Serial No.267 Sands Hotel
                                        Dymchurch

        as per telephone cobversation.

iver's copy of this order to be delivered to the Receiving Depot with aircraft)

                                Superintendent,C.S.O.
                                No.49 Maintenance Unit,R.A.F.
                                at Faygate,Horsham, Sussex

This was the official 49 MU Enemy Aircraft Collection Order issued to A.V. Nicholls & Co. with instructions to remove the remains of the Bexley Dornier and convey to RAF Faygate.

An unusual assignment for the RAF Maintenance Unit salvage parties was for the removal of a number of Italian aircraft shot down over the East Coast when the Italian air force attempted a mass daylight raid on Harwich on 11 November 1940. A number of Fiat CR.42 bi-plane fighters and Fiat BR.20 bombers were shot down, including this Fiat CR.42 which ended up on its nose on a shingle beach at Orfordness and provided a good picture opportunity for a news photographer. This aircraft was removed intact, repaired and test flown by the RAF. Unlike its Me 110 counterpart from Hawkhurst, this aircraft survived the war and actually *did* end up in the RAF Museum at Hendon.

Another of the Italian raiders that came to grief was this further example of a Fiat CR.42 down at Corton Railway Station near Lowestoft on the same day, although in rather a worse state than the CR.42 at Orfordness. This raid was a complete failure, was costly to the Italian Air Force, and was never repeated.

Yet another of the Italian raiding force was this Fiat BR.20 bomber that came to grief in Rendlesham Forest near Woodbridge, Suffolk. Already badly smashed, the only way to extricate this bomber was for the RAF salvage party to further break it up and drag it from the trees. Already souvenir hunters have been to work and cut out the emblems at the top of the white crosses on the rudders.

Price 3d.

To be Sold in Aid of the Royal Air Force Benevolent Fund.

THE SALVAGE MAN'S SONG.

By L. A. C. Gray.

We'll all drink a toast to the lads in the sky,
The pilots, observers, and gunners who fly,
But fill up your glasses, another toast yet,
We'll drink to the men we sometimes forget,
To the lads who are doing a useful job too,
To the scrap iron men of the salvage M.U.

They are not very smart—their trousers aren't pressed,
They seldom get time to go out in their best,
Their usual workshop a forest or fen,
A seashore or cornfield, a mountain or glen,
But whenever an aeroplane goes for a " Burton,"
Wherever it is, they will get it—for certain.

Sometimes in a swamp, a 'plane they will find,
And what with the mud, it's a bit of a " bind,"
The job's seldom done without some kind of hitch,
You can gamble that most of it's stuck in a ditch,
But with mud to the eyebrows, they'll get out that 'plane,
And off on a loader to be fixed up again.

When icy winds blow, and snow's on the deck,
They are still just as keen to salvage a wreck,
They pick up Italians, Jerries, or Dutch,
And though sometimes they " brown-off " they don't grumble (much)
They billet at farmhouses, pubs, or a 'drome,
Wherever a crash, it's their temporary home.

And when Summer comes, and it's hot, no one shirks,
They're pretty tough fellows, those scrap iron " erks,"
There are Flight Mechs., and Riggers, and Fitters IIE,
And the cream of them all, the good old M.T.
Whatever the time, they answer the call,
We all know their motto, and that's—BLESS 'EM ALL?

So fill up your glasses and drink to the chaps
Who work in the background, and pick up the scraps,
To build us new " kites "—make us new guns,
To finish off Adolf, and give Hell to the Huns.
So empty your glasses, and loosen your collars,
Give three hearty cheers for those salvage wallahs.

At some stage after the arrival of these Italian aircraft LAC Grey, an airman with an RAF Maintenance Unit salvage party, penned this 'Salvage Man's Song' and had the short ditty published to raise funds for the RAF Benevolent Fund. A clue as to the date lies in reference to Italian aircraft, and the words reflect the wry humour of the salvage crews as they faced their often thankless and arduous tasks. Most of the scenarios Grey mentions in these verses have been more than extensively covered in the photo content of this book and will be recognised by readers.

Another unusual aircraft type was this RAF Martin Maryland medium bomber of the Overseas Air Movement Control Unit from RAF Kemble which stalled on take-off from RAF Tangmere on 25 February 1941 and is photographed here as a salvage party from RAF Faygate's 49 MU get to work on its removal. Flying Officer R.J.S. Wooton and his crew escaped, although one of them was injured.

A relatively unusual Luftwaffe aircraft type to be brought down over England was the Dornier 215. This example was shot down at Eaton Socon in Bedfordshire on 24 October 1940 and is being guarded by a War Reserve Constable before inspection by an RAF Intelligence Officer. As the Blitz gathered momentum after 7 September 1940, so the scale of downed fighters decreased, and the majority of Luftwaffe aircraft that were being destroyed became bombers.

Another Dornier, but this time a Dornier 17, was shattered when it met its demise at Boconnoc Estate near Lostwithiel in Cornwall on 9 November 1940 killing all four crew. Hitting the ground at a shallow angle the aircraft careered into woodland and exploded, leaving little for this fed-up looking RAF airman to guard or for the Maintenance Unit salvage parties to later clear up. Usually the recovery gangs cleared debris away with a remarkable thoroughness, although in this instance a group of enthusiasts, searching forty years later for scattered parts of the Dornier, found three unexploded 50kg bombs in the undergrowth.

With the number of Spitfires being collected by 49 MU it would seem that every penny raised for the Spitfire Fund would have been much needed. Here, Sgt Cyril Babbage's 602 Squadron Spitfire has come a cropper during a wheels-down emergency landing at Iford Hill near Lewes, East Sussex on 12 October 1940. Having run through a hedge, the Spitfire flipped onto its back after the wheels hit a small ditch. Although quite badly damaged, the aircraft was repairable.

Perhaps faring a little worse was this Spitfire of 66 Squadron (X4255) that had been hit by British anti-aircraft fire over the South Coast on 11 October 1940, forcing Pilot Officer H.R. 'Dizzy' Allen to execute an emergency landing at RAF Hawkinge. The aircraft ran through the perimeter fence and barbed-wire, ending up looking rather the worse for wear and with its pilot suffering from concussion. Remarkably, and despite the extensive damage shown here, the aircraft was repaired and returned to service with 53 Operational Training Unit although fate once again took a hand when an engine failure resulted in another forced landing, near Llantwit Major in Wales on 15 June 1942. This time the Spitfire was written off after running through a hedge.

Safely onto its Queen Mary trailer, 'Dizzy' Allen's Spitfire is headed for a repair depot, via 49 MU at Faygate, as two of the salvage party strike the almost obligatory pose with their latest 'job'. The truck's identity plate clearly indicates that the vehicle is on the inventory of 49 Maintenance Unit.

A bandaged Flt Lt Geoffrey Matheson of 222 Squadron surveys the burnt-out remnants of his Spitfire after he had crash-landed near the Sittingbourne Paper Mills on 30 August 1940. The aircraft has exploded shortly after Matheson got the battle-damaged Spitfire on the ground and he was lucky to escape with relatively minor wounds.

This Spitfire of 92 Squadron had come to grief after crashing into one of the buildings at RAF Biggin Hill and it became another routine wreck collection job for the teams from RAF Faygate. Not every aircraft loss during wartime was directly related to war operations or combat; many crashes had been the result of pilot error, mechanical failure, the weather or through navigational mistakes.

(*Above*) Seemingly in rather better condition is this Hurricane at RAF Biggin Hill as LAC Don Booth's salvage party from 49 MU, RAF Faygate, prepare to dismantle and remove it from the airfield. Booth is second left, wearing the tin helmet. He had obviously heard about the frequent air attacks to which Biggin Hill had been subjected! Almost certainly the Hurricane shown here was being removed for repair prior to a likely return to service.

(*Opposite above*) Into the Blitz, and Luftwaffe bomber aircraft continued to fall the length and breadth of the British Isles. Often they were in the most inaccessible of locations. Here, for example, a Heinkel 111 was shot down into the Thames Estuary on the night of 15/16 January 1941 off Canvey Island. It has been 'caught' by a port authority vessel and is slowly being edged ashore for examination by RAF Intelligence Officers and eventual scrapping. Aircraft that were lost at sea were rarely recovered, or recoverable.

(*Opposite below*) Posing equally challenging salvage problems was this Junkers 88 that had plummeted into marshland at Banks Marsh, Southport, Lancashire, on the night of 7/8 April 1941. Two of the crew had baled out and were taken prisoner, whilst the remaining two were killed in the crash. Here an RAF Crash Inspector from an RAF Maintenance Unit examines the tail unit and ponders how, or if, it might be recovered. Abandonment due to impracticalities of recovery was often the only option and a great deal of wreckage was abandoned to the marshes in this instance.

Another tail unit, but this time from a Blenheim that has crashed and burned out near RAF Manston, Kent. The 49 MU salvage party again pose for the customary group photograph before the wreckage is loaded up for return to Faygate. This was not a wreck that could be repaired or returned to service and was described as 'Category 3' damage – i.e. written-off.

And again, on that same theme of aircraft tail units, another one is inspected at its crash site at Vaasetter on Fair Isle in the Shetlands. The aircraft is a Heinkel 111 of a weather reconnaissance unit that had crashed there on 18 January 1941. Recovery was deemed impossible and the wreck was still in situ at least until very recent years. When this photograph was taken, not too long after the crash, islanders have already stripped sheets of alloy from the wreck – this was probably not for souvenirs but more likely to be for some practical use, perhaps in the repair of roofs and outhouses in this meteorologically inhospitable place.

Less challenging than the Southport wreck was a Junkers 88 shot down at Poling, West Sussex on 24 March 1941. In this shot, it is still burning shortly after crashing at Parsons Farm but the bomber was swiftly removed to RAF Faygate not very many miles away from the crash site. Perhaps because a fresh supply of German aircraft wrecks was rather drying up this Junkers was earmarked for display purposes.

This is the very same Junkers 88 some months later after being transported to the Corn Exchange, Brighton, for a War Weapons Exhibition. Although on an RAF Queen Mary, Mr Arthur Nicholls of A.V. Nicholls & Co. greets the wreck in his capacity as Mayor of Brighton and stands in his homburg hat flanked by two RAF airmen. By this stage of the war his company was no longer involved in wreck recovery, the task having been taken over by the establishment of 86 Maintenance Unit at Sundridge. This must have seemed like a busman's holiday for Arthur Nicholls.

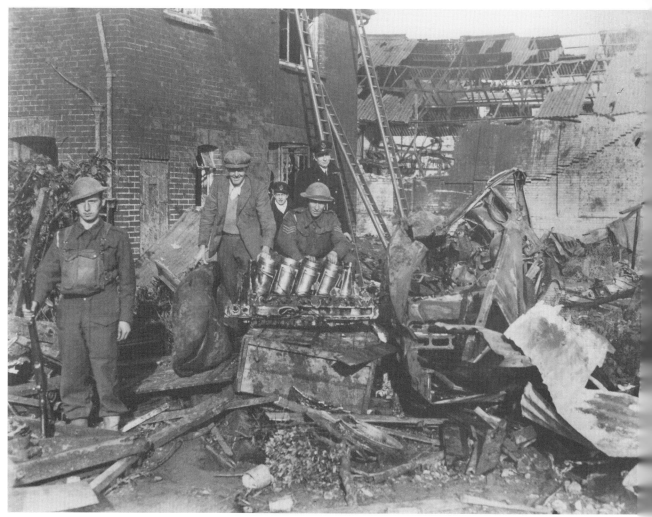

(*Above*) Rather more beaten up was this Luftwaffe Blitz victim, a Junkers 88 that had crashed and exploded on Moore's Garage, Ringwood Road, Poole on 14 November after being shot down by Spitfires of 152 Squadron. Mangled wreckage and an engine can be seen here, mixed in with rubble and debris from the demolished garage. The clear up process has already begun, but the German bomber has almost totally disintegrated in the impact and subsequent fire.

(*Opposite page*) Also in Dorset, and just down the coast, on 22 May 1941, this He 111 H-8 of 4./KG27 (1G+ZM, W.Nr 3974) hit the top of a mist covered hill during a sortie to Yeovil, Somerset, and crashed at Chideock Farm, Chaldon Herring at 21.04 hours. One 500kg and two 250kg bombs were still on board. Oblt F. Bartels, Ofw H. Hahn, and Ofw H. Grimmel all landed safely with the aircraft, but Ofw H. Funk and Gefr K. Kohler baled out too low and both were killed. The aircraft was removed to Royal Aircraft Establishment Farnborough for detailed examination of the balloon fender which, at a weight of 550lbs, proved too cumbersome for operational use and the remaining thirty or so H-3 and H-5 aircraft that had been modified to the H-8 were eventually stripped of the fender and re-designated He 111 H-8/R2 glider tugs. Also shown is the same unusual aircraft after partial dismantling by the RAF salvage party, a photograph taken sneakily (and illegally) past the sentry's rifle by a private photographer!

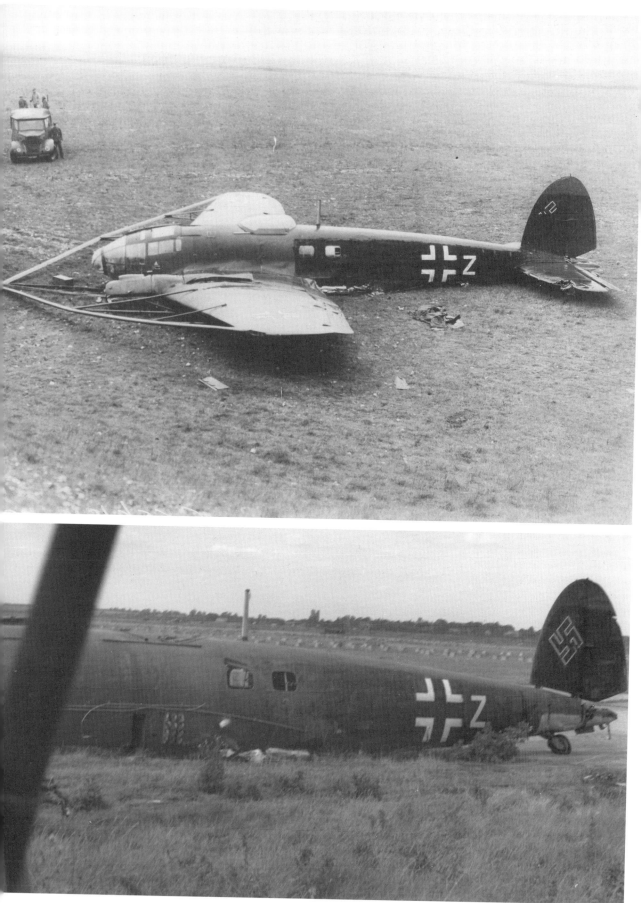

(*Above*) Although the 'Messerschmitt 109 harvest' from the previous summer and autumn had slowed, a few examples of the type continued to fall over Britain during the winter of 1940 and into the early part of 1941. Here, a novel means of extracting Lt Otto Zauner's aircraft of II./JG53 is found by a 49 Maintenance Unit salvage party as two cart horses are harnessed to the fuselage in what is a classic photograph from the period. Zauner had had a lucky escape in this crash on 23 November 1940 when his stricken Messerschmitt narrowly passed under power cables near Smeeth Railway Station in Kent and then careered on through some trees where it smashed off both wings before coming to rest, with a shaken but unharmed Otto Zauner still in the cockpit.

(*Opposite above*) Another Luftwaffe Blitz loss was this Heinkel 111 of 9./KG26 that broke up in mid-air after being attacked by a Defiant night fighter at Bendish, near Hitchin in Hertfordshire on the night of 8/9 April 1941. Three of the crew managed to bale out safely, but a fourth was killed. Here, three soldiers guard the broken wing tip of the Heinkel which has very comprehensively reduced itself to scrap. What little else was left was also badly broken up and burnt. Yet more alloy for the smelters and eventual raw material for the British Ministry of Aircraft Production.

(*Opposite below*) By the Spring of 1941 a new Maintenance Unit, Number 86, was fully established at Sundridge, near Sevenoaks in Kent, to help deal with the litter of aircraft wrecks across southern England, and its formation resulted in the stand-down of Air Ministry civilian contractors like A.V. Nicholls & Co. Here, an unidentified RAF airman poses with a smashed wing section outside one of the huts at the 86 MU site of RAF Sundridge, Kent, during the early part of 1941.

(*Above*) Two of the RAF salvage party are photographed with three of the MG 17 machine guns from Rudolf Hess's Messerschmitt 110 in a specially posed 'H for Hess' arrangement, a picture that was reproduced in many newspapers and journals of the period.

(*Opposite page*) There can be little or no doubt that the bizarre arrival in Scotland of Hitler's deputy, Rudolf Hess, in a Messerschmitt 110 on 10 May 1941 presented the RAF Maintenance Units with their most unusual and high-profile job as they collected the pieces of smashed wreckage from the crash site on Bonnyton Moor, Eaglesham, a few miles south-west of Glasgow. Here, the wreckage is scattered across a meadow at Floor Farm.

(*Opposite below*) Later, the jumbled wreckage was deposited at a nearby railway goods yard and comes under scrutiny from two RAF officers and an officer from a Scottish regiment.

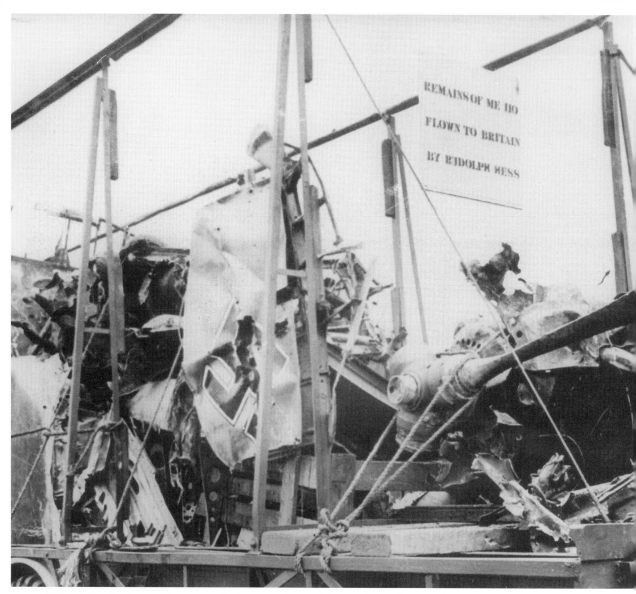

REMAINS OF ME 110
FLOWN TO BRITAIN
BY RUDOLPH HESS

(*Above*) Finally the wreckage was piled onto a Queen Mary trailer and moved down to Southern England where it was initially exhibited as shown here. The fuselage and engines were preserved for museum display and today comprise a major Imperial War Museum exhibit.

(*Opposite above*) This photograph shows one of the RAF's Intelligence Officers at work, as Flight Lieutenant Michael Golovine inspects what is left of a Junkers 88 shot down on 20 November 1940 at Stocks Lane, East Wittering, West Sussex. Golovine noted bullet and cannon strikes in the wreckage, and one of those holes is visible in the spar just below and to the left of his right hand. A schoolboy stands fascinated by the spectacle and a water-filled crater, off to the right, hides the buried wreckage of most of the bomber. Again, very little for 49 MU to cart away.

(*Opposite below*) This slightly older schoolboy, meanwhile, is no doubt wondering if he can sneak off with this trophy before the men of 49 Maintenance Unit arrive from RAF Faygate. He is examining the aircraft's tail wheel assembly, but unfortunately he needs to find something rather smaller to fit in in his coat pocket!

(*Above*) When Pilot Officer Armstrong of 74 Squadron was shot down in his Spitfire over Sandwich, Kent on 14 November 1940 he baled out leaving his aircraft to bury itself deep in the ground at Bellers Bush Farm where it became another job for the boys from A.V. Nicholls & Co. Here, Jack Austin burrows deep into the soil as the gang dig down to the engine which they reached at fourteen feet but were unable to extricate it from the soft ground and were forced to abandon it.

(*Opposite page*) Another job for RAF Intelligence Officers as they survey the wreckage of a Dornier 17–Z of 2./Kustenfliegergruppe 606 that had taken off from its base near Brest to attack Liverpool on 16 October 1940. It is believed that the aircraft lost its bearings and ran out fuel before crashing at Masbury Ring near Wells in Somerset at around 23.55 hours. However the wreck was not found until mid-day on 17 October, the bodies of the four crew and ten 50kg bombs being scattered amongst the widely dispersed wreckage. Here, one RAF officer takes notes as another peers at an engine. When their job was finished, the intelligence experts could 'release' the wreckage for removal.

(*Above*) It was not until October 2011 that the engine was finally dug out as part of a series of military history wreck-recovery programmes for the Discovery History Channel. Here, the Rolls Royce Merlin engine that the Nicholls gang were forced to abandon is finally brought up.

(*Opposite above*) Whilst the numbers of Messerschmitt 109 being brought down over the UK had drastically diminished by the early part of 1941 due to the cessation of fighter-escorted bomber raids, an exception was the arrival of this one in July 1941. In fact this was the very first example captured intact by the RAF of the Messerschmitt 109-F variant, and was an extremely valuable prize. The aircraft had been hit in the radiator over the English Channel and disabled. The pilot, a leading Luftwaffe ace, Hptm Rolf Pingel, made a forced landing and was taken prisoner before he could destroy his aircraft. Here it is shown being lifted from its crash location at St Margaret's Bay, near Dover, by the men from 49 MU and their trusty Coles crane after the Messerschmitt's arrival there on 10 July 1941.

(*Opposite below*) In this photograph, the Messerschmitt 109-F is seen at the Royal Aircraft Establishment, Farnborough, where it underwent repairs and was test flown by the RAF in British camouflage and marking, although it ultimately crashed near Fowlmere, Cambridgeshire whilst being tested, which resulted in the death of its Polish pilot. It was thought that the cause of the fatal crash was carbon monoxide poisoning caused by leakage into the cockpit of exhaust gasses.

Finds like this German Junkers Jumo aero engine are sometimes pulled up in trawl nets. This example was brought ashore at Hastings during the late 1960s.

And this was a Messerschmitt 109 that had been shot down on 7 October 1940 being pulled out of the sea by the Brenzett Aeronautical Museum during the 1970s. Notwithstanding the sterling efforts of the military and civilian crash salvage parties during the war years it is inevitable that aircraft wrecks they left behind will still be found for many years yet, especially inaccessible crashes such as these in coastal waters.